BEIJING TIME

Harvard University Press

Cambridge, Massachusetts   London, England   2008

BEIJING TIME

MICHAEL DUTTON

Hsiu-ju Stacy Lo   Dong Dong Wu

Library of Congress Cataloging-in-Publication Data
Dutton, Michael Robert.
    Beijing time / Michael Dutton, Hsiu-ju Stacy Lo, Dong Dong Wu.
    p. cm.
    ISBN 978-0-674-02789-3
1. Beijing (China)—Description and travel. I. Lo, Hsiu-ju Stacy, 1983–
II. Wu, Dong Dong, 1961– III. Title.
    DS795.D88 2008
    951'.156—dc22
    2007038348

This book is dedicated to my father,
Robert Munro Dutton, from whom I
have learned so much about life and
for whom I hope I am not too late to
give a little life back. MD

CONTENTS

MAPS

BEIJING TIME

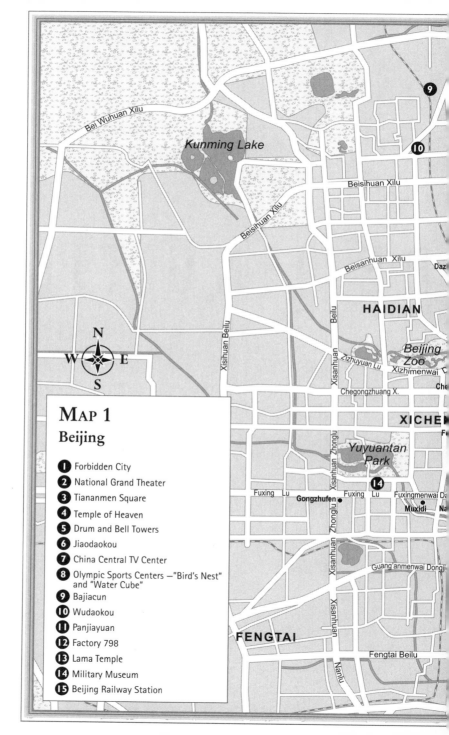

MAP 1
Beijing

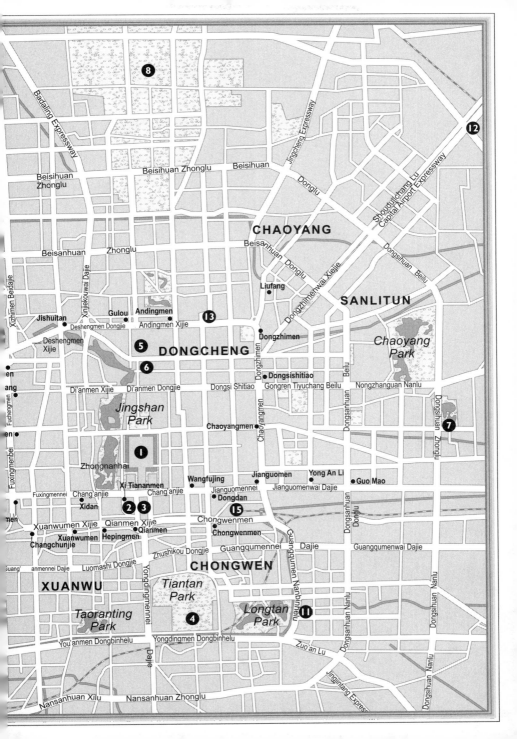

1   THE SQUARE

It's four o'clock on a freezing autumn morning in Beijing. An eerie silence hangs over the city. Predawn Beijing is nothing if not surreal. No cars, no people, no crowds. Beijing without its teeming millions is hard to imagine, yet at this time of day it's a reality. That is, of course, unless you venture into the heart of this city, Tiananmen Square. Here, in the auroral light, an even more surreal event is about to shatter the morning silence. Among the crowded silhouettes of thousands of shivering souls from across this nation, anticipation hangs in the air. Stretching and yawning, they have made their way to this early-morning scene to watch dawn break and to witness the daily reenactment of the birth of the Chinese nation. On the recently repaved granite surface of the square, crack troops from the sixty-strong National Flag-Raising Brigade of the People's Armed Police begin their daily ritual. As they raise the flag to the rousing sound of the national anthem, the heart of every Chinese present begins to pound.

Day in, day out, thousands of Chinese tourists from across the country come here to participate in this event and, in so doing, to reaffirm their own sense of national belonging. Perversely, it is tourism that has revived this once-forgotten ceremony.[1] These days, the ceremony is the must-see item on any Chinese tourist itinerary of the capital. All Chinese tours begin here, and joining these throngs, viewing this ceremony and the people's responses to it, makes it easier to appreciate the power of nation in the contemporary Chinese imagination and also the central role of Beijing and Tiananmen Square in that reimagining of nationhood.

In Tiananmen Square we are surrounded by potent symbols of nationhood. As the awe-inspiring sounds of the national anthem slice through the pronounced silence of predawn Tiananmen, all are moved. After the ceremony, the tourists board their buses and are transported to the outskirts of the city, where they visit powerful symbols of Beijing's ancient greatness. At the Great Wall they gaze with wonder at a relic of the genius of their forebears, before moving on to the Ming tombs to pay homage to the ancestral founders of Beijing.

This is a city haunted by memories of greatness, extending from dynastic times, through the creation of New China in 1949, to the status as a postmodern global hub that is central to its identity today. Architecturally and spatially, Beijing incorporates many different layers and times, acknowledged and unacknowledged. While it continues to grow and to experience spectacular refashionings today, Beijing is also a museum, capturing centuries of Chinese nationhood.

It was perhaps the ability of this city to carry within itself these different layers and meanings that led China's foremost architect of the modern era, Liang Sicheng, to say of this city that it was an "unparalleled masterpiece" that should be protected.[2] It is perhaps for similar reasons that Liang's son, Liang Congjie, now objects to one of the central city's biggest redevelopment plans, the construction of the massive Oriental Plaza on one of the main shopping boulevards, Wangfujing.[3] If the younger Liang objects to the wholesale destruction of the city, he does so because of the rapacious free-market capitalism of the post-Mao era. For the older Liang, the main threat to the preservation of the city's past lay in the politically inspired destruction he felt might accompany the Communist Party's determination to overcome ancient customs and old habits. Fearing that plans to redevelop Beijing as a socialist capital would endanger the unique and ancient layer of this urban environment, Liang called upon the Party to protect the older suburbs by building a new socialist center to the west of the city. His pleas fell on deaf ears. Indeed, as the noted architect Chen Gan points out, the minute the flag of New China was raised in Tiananmen Square to commemorate the founding of the People's Republic, Liang's conception was already a dead letter.[4] The result was a Soviet-inspired socialist transformation of the urban landscape that would mark Beijing as profoundly as the dynastic rulers

1   Tiananmen Square, where all Chinese tours begin.

2   One of the square's many vendors.

had done before the Communist Revolution. That socialist Beijing has, itself, begun to disappear. Indeed, as the Hong Kong cultural critic Chen Guanzhong observes, the post-economic-reform Beijing is now a "bohemian capital."[5]

Bohemian Beijing marks out another side to this city and flags the fact that the city has become far less somber, far less conservative, and more funloving than before. Contemporary Beijing is also far more experimental and open to an avant-garde than either the dynastic or socialist city it is built upon. The architecture of this new city is no less spectacular than that of the past even if it carries within it a very different meaning. From Rem Koolhaas and Ole Scheeren's China Central Television (CCTV) Headquarters Building and Cultural Center, to the new National Grand Theater of Paul Andreu, to the new postmodern architectural forms of the various Olympic venues, the city sparkles. Yet it isn't just architecture that is renewing this place. Increasingly, this is a city filled with an exciting and hedonistic nightlife in places such as Gongti, Houhai, and Sanlitun. It includes revamped shopping areas such as Wangfujing, Xidan, and Guomao, as well as suburbs like Wudaokou, which are filled with coffee shops and salon bookshops exemplifying this new, more materialist world. If the raising of the new nation's flag in Tiananmen in 1949 was central to an earlier phase of city and national reconstruction, it is the flag of consumerism that, as in every other major city in China, hangs over Beijing's reconstruction projects of today. The city is booming, and the cityscape reflects this fact. Gleaming new buildings that are design statements bump up against fabulous new shopping malls that sell individualized examples of the same sort of fashion statement. Every store is awash with chic consumer goods. From top-line imports to knock-off fashion accessories, from the most recent imported consumer gadgets to the latest Hollywood blockbuster burnt onto a cheap pirated DVD, Beijing shops and markets offer every conceivable consumer item at every conceivable price.

An entire generation has now grown up on these things and developed its own unique mentality based on the world of which it is a part. While only a few have had access to "authentic" top brands, just about every city kid on the street has had a chance to buy a knockoff CD. Indeed, so ubiquitous are the kids who have been breast-fed on pirated Western music that they have become known not as generation X, but as the saw-gash generation.

"Saw-gash" is the term used to describe the small punch hole that Western record companies cut into their excess CDs before shipping them off as waste for disposal in far-off China. The "gash" cut into the CD was designed to make the music unplayable and the disk unsellable. What the record companies hadn't reckoned upon were the ingenuity of Chinese entrepreneurs and the willingness of young Chinese consumers to forgo the pleasures of the last track. For the relatively poor Chinese consumer, saw-gash CDs were but one spoke in a set of trainer wheels teaching the young about Western consumer culture and cultural taste. Collectively, pirated goods became a crucial device in translating Western culture and transforming the Chinese socialist value system. With pirated products and fake brands, even the poorest of urban Chinese could afford to take part in the new consumer world at the fashionable top end.

Among members of the saw-gash generation, the songs they fix upon, the categories they use to organize their musical tastes, the way they respond to the music all bear an uncanny likeness to their Western counterparts, yet in small but significant ways they are incongruous. Nevertheless, the globalization of refuse disposal has transformed Western trash into a cheap Chinese treasure that has played a crucial cultural role in transforming a new generation.

When we realize the power of such products not just to find a place in the market, but to redefine culture, we realize that to begin to appreciate China it is necessary to look not only at national treasures but also at its trash. We will do just that when we venture out to the town of Bajiacun, one of the many "trash cities" existing precariously on the outskirts of Beijing. We will also be looking through the secondhand fashion shops of nearby Wudaokou and spending time with budding artists and movie directors in one of the chic salons that now dot that suburban landscape. For the moment, however, it is simply enough to note the importance of the role of this consumer market in the redevelopment of this city. Arguably more than any single change in the law or political move by the central government, consumerism has profoundly transformed this nation, this city, and its people. It has changed everything, from people's habits right through to the urban landscape.

The rise and spread of the new consumer mentality and the wealth it has generated have endangered the labyrinth of traditional gray compound houses that once characterized central Beijing. The sheer size of the urban population meant that the only way to go was up, in high-rise dwellings. Today, in more traditional suburbs, older people speak with mixed feelings about "going upstairs" *(shang lou)*—a new colloquialism coined to describe high-rise living. For many, this is more than a move from one house to another; it is a move out of one mode of living and into another, more "modern" one. Residents of the old compound houses who have moved into new high-rise apartments might genuinely feel a loss of community, but at least they now have inside toilets and hot running water. Old Beijing might feel a profound sense of spiritual loss, but it also recognizes the material compensations of this new way of life.

The almost religious dedication that was once shown to Mao's "three loyalties" *(san zhongyu)* during the Cultural Revolution—loyalty to Mao, to the Party, and to socialism—gave way to a new form of materialism that, by the beginning of the 1980s, had turned devotion to the three loyalties into a desire for the "three wheels" *(sanzhuan)*—a bicycle, a sewing machine, and a watch. These were, however, simply the first markers of a new and nascent form of market-based consumerism that helped erode a collectivized mind-set fixated upon politics. The key aspirations today, the "four haves" *(siyou)*—an apartment, a car, a good facial, and a great body—mark an inflation of desires.

This new aspirational culture has not only demolished older mind-sets but obliterated entire neighborhoods of compound houses and old socialist-style apartments. Nietzsche once claimed that great leaders of the future would philosophize with a hammer. In Beijing, they would do so with a jackhammer. Whole neighborhoods disappeared, and in their place arose new luxury high-rise apartments, shopping arcades, and business districts. Demolition took place at such a rate that, at one stage in the 1990s, Beijing was, like many urban regions of China, a city of *chai*. The character *chai*, meaning "to demolish," was so widespread that it became one of the most recognized characters throughout China. Even art picked up on its importance; every second building marked for destruction seemed to have this character scrawled across its walls. "Buildings are being knocked down at such a rate that one doesn't even have time to film them anymore," complained one cultural critic, Song Xiaoxia.[6] Yet it wasn't just the speed of change that created his feeling of unease. What followed the demolition proved to be even more disorienting.

Out of this culture of rapid change emerged a new generation of young pioneers very different from their socialist predecessors. These youngsters were no longer striving to realize socialism; they were too busy exploring and playing with the phantasmagorical possibilities opened up by China's new consumer culture. From the delights of virtual reality, through the emergence of punk rock, to the development of avant-garde art colonies such as 798, Beijing was changing its landscape just as its people were changing their old mentality. Cool cafés and funky bars materialized in the gray cityscape of the older socialist Beijing. These new venues opened onto a very different city and mind-set from the one dominated by the passion for politics of the Mao era or by the sobriety of dynastic times.

More than ever before, Beijing has become a city where just beneath the surface we discover many different layers of space and time. We get a glimpse of these layers as we travel farther from Tiananmen Square. Yet the square remains the essential starting point for any such journey.

The shadow of Tiananmen is not the shadow summoned up for Westerners by recollections of the event of 4 June 1989. When Chinese tourists gather at dawn in the square, they are not revisiting a shattering televised image of a young man facing down a government tank. Instead, the clockwork precision of the flagraising, the inspirational national anthem, the drills of crack soldiers combine to beat out a message of national pride, not national shame. Tiananmen has become the reenactment of nationhood; it is the glorious place where New China was proclaimed, and from where a very different China is now arising. Indeed, some Chinese scholars have suggested that this will be the nation leading the way in the Asia Pacific region and possibly the world in the twenty-first century.[7]

At the dawn of a new century, many believe that China's time has arrived, and Beijing captures that timeline, for it is at the very heart of things Chinese. Yet history continues to tick away in the background. Listening carefully to these other timepieces, we discover other ways in which Beijing is in a time, and a world, of its own. Yet it is a time and a world not wholly its own.

The name Martial Bourdin will mean nothing to any China expert, yet in many ways it is through the fictionalized account of this French anarchist's final day on earth that we can catch a glimpse of the logic underlying the Chinese revolution that transformed Beijing into the nation's timekeeper. Bourdin was the figure upon whom Joseph Conrad based the character of Mr. Verloc in his novel *The Secret Agent*. In Conrad's hands, the death of the hapless anarchist in the park at Greenwich became the basis of an absurd, almost comical, plot to blow up time itself by blowing up the Royal Observatory. It was as though the attempt to blow up the prime

3   Wang Jinsong's collage of the character *chai*, meaning "to demolish."

4   The 798 Café: old socialism and new chic.

meridian was an effort to destroy the very logic by which the entire capitalist system adjusted its watch.

Revolutionary change has always been linked to overturning time. Who can forget the ticking clock in that classic movie of the Russian Revolution, Eisenstein's *October?* As midnight approached, so too did the Bolsheviks. The storming of the Summer Palace was but one shot away. And who can forget tales of the French revolutionary calendar, which began with a bang on day one of Year One, when citizens reportedly fired upon the clocks of Paris? By the 1970s, of course, it was not clocks but people that the brutal Khmer Rouge were firing upon as they rewound their timepieces back to year zero. The Chinese Communists also played with time, though in a far less spectacular fashion. Without linking change to revolutionary romanticism or to a brutal program of class eradication, the Chinese Communist Party nevertheless revealed, in its play on time, a new order of concerns that would come to anchor its new world order.

When the Communist Party newspaper, the *People's Daily,* hit the newsstands on 28 September 1949, its masthead date was rendered not in the calendrical time of the Middle Kingdom but in that of the Gregorian calendar. Wedged between two epochal events, this change might well have been missed by readers. If so, there were good reasons for missing it. On 21 September 1949 the paper had printed Mao's famous speech in which he announced that the Chinese people had finally "stood up"; on 1 October it would publish the historic declaration, emanating from Tiananmen Gate (the Gate of Heavenly Peace), announcing the establishment of the People's Republic of China (PRC).

Between these two momentous events, who would have noticed the change in the paper's masthead revealing that the Communist Party had, in effect, switched from one method of calculating time to another? This switch set the establishment of the People's Republic not in "the thirty-eighth year of the Republic" or even in the "first year of the People's Republic." Instead it became, quite simply, the Revolution of '49. Science and modernization were a key part of this revolution, and the abandonment of the lunar calendar in favor of the Gregorian one marked this affiliation. Yet the Party's nationalist desire to modernize could not take place without unification of the country, and one other revolutionary time change made this desire for unification abundantly clear.

The 1949 declaration of nationhood not only announced Beijing as the new capital, replacing the old Nationalist capital of Nanjing; it also made this new capital the nation's time lord. From five time zones before the revolution, China became just one. As Communist rule extended across the vastness from Tibet in the west to Hainan Island in the east, all the nation's clocks were adjusted to reflect the new reality of unification. Beijing time now ruled throughout China (except, of course, in Taiwan). This collapsing of multiple time zones into one was no pragmatic exercise to appease a farming lobby or maximize daylight. It was a political decision to centralize all decision-making, including those about time, in Beijing and in the hands of the Party's Central Committee; appropriately, it was called Beijing Time *(Beijing shijian)*. Thus from 1949 onward China would awaken and rise to the ticktock of Party time, and that meant time would always be closely associated with struggle.

This revolutionary ticktock from Beijing also set the alarm clocks of the class struggles that dominated China from 1949 right through to 1979. In effect the nation's history was divided into only two temporal zones, and they were entirely political. One of these, referred to as "before liberation" *(jiefang qian)*, was irredeemably bad; the other, referred to as "after liberation" *(jiefang hou)*, was wholly good. Neither the adoption of the Gregorian calendar nor the unification of time zones adequately captures this new revolutionary temporality. This historic divide between "before liberation" and "after liberation" still persists in common usage, although these expressions have become routinized and are largely free of their original political potency. In the decades just after the revolution, however, the full political import of every syllable in these phrases was still pronounced.

For those who spoke of what they had endured before the revolution, there is little doubt that this temporal divide was more than Party propaganda. We will see this for ourselves when we bear witness to some of these tales of bitterness articulated in passing by elderly residents of the Beijing suburb of Jiaodaokou. For now, it is enough to note that contrary to the claims of Cold Warriors and critics of contemporary China, the Communist Party didn't just kill its enemies; it also brought new life to the city and to its "friends," the "people." It is this side of the Tiananmen story that speaks to Chinese tourists who come to Tiananmen Square at dawn and still preface their remarks about China with the phrase "after liberation."

Like the square itself, these expressions are a revolutionary timepiece, recalling events that once shook China and heralded a new beginning for the nation. The new beginning was inextricably linked to the project of nation building, modernization, and socialism, and it was in Tiananmen Square more than anywhere else in China that this new imagining was given a physical form.

That Tiananmen Square was the epicenter of this new national mythology is attested by the fact that the first postrevolutionary dollar note issued by the new Chinese Central Bank featured Tiananmen Gate.[8] The note was originally to have featured Mao Zedong, whose enlarged portrait had by then replaced Chiang Kaishek's above Tiananmen Gate itself; but the Chairman himself vetoed that idea. Rather surprisingly, given the subsequent cult of personality, Mao suggested that "people's money" *(renminbi)* belonged to the people and should reflect that fact. Working overtime to implement Mao's wishes, designers selected Tiananmen Gate, minus Mao's portrait, as the best symbol of the new unity of the people. By then, the linkage established between the center of the city and the revolution doomed any prospects of preserving the old city intact. As one of the architects central to the 1950s redesign of Tiananmen Square made clear, "when the picture of Tiananmen became the most important symbol of the People's Republic of China, a mission to change the ancient city fell on the shoulders of the city planners."[9]

Indeed, Tiananmen had already become the people's square with the decision, taken just hours before the formal 1 October 1949 declaration of the founding of the PRC, to build at the center of the square a "Monument to the People's Heroes."[10] As a result of concerns about symbolism that dovetailed with those already evident in the debate about the appropriate iconography for New China's money, the building of the monument would be delayed by wrangling until Labor Day 1958. In the interim, architects, Party theorists, and spatial planners debated not just the shape, style, and orientation of the monument but also the future role of the city. Was Beijing to remain a city that hallowed its ancient origins, or was it to be transformed into a showcase of a modern socialist life? As it turned out, the monument became the first peg in the ground of this new socialist city.

The classical cosmology of old Beijing ordained that everything must face south; the Monument to the People's Heroes faced north. Traditional concerns about the flow of the life-affirming spirit (qi) demanded that the south-north axis of the city be open to facilitate this flow; the new monument interrupted it. The epicenter of the old Beijing had been the Forbidden City; the new arrangement relocated that center at the foot of the monument. The structure marked a revolutionary reorientation of the city, one followed by a whole set of minirevolutions in planning and building that reinforced the symbolic relocation of the city center to Tiananmen Square.[11]

Liang Sicheng, the chief architect of the monument, described it as "socialist in content and national in form." The design was modeled on a traditional Chinese stele but featured on its main northern face a saying by Mao Zedong, written in his own hand: "Eternal Glory to the People's Heroes."[12] The monument not only faced north; it also was inordinately tall. Unlike traditional steles, the structure rose 37.94 meters, dwarfing even Tiananmen Gate immediately to its north. Liang Sicheng considered the traditional stele simply too short, too gloomy, and too lifeless to reflect adequately the real spirit of struggle among the people.[13]

Parading in chronological sequence around the 40.68-meter base of the monument is a series of sculpted 2-meter-high marble panels.[14] Beginning with the burning of British opium in 1840 and culminating in the Communists' guerrilla struggle against Japanese imperialists in the 1940s, the scenes portray Mao Zedong's view of modern Chinese history as one long struggle by the people against imperialist aggression.[15] Most striking about these scenes of collective revolutionary action is the absence of a great and beloved leader making history. This is history without an individual subject; it is the tale of mass, anonymous, and heroic struggle— the struggle for national liberation.

5   Signage from the epicenter.

6   The first postrevolutionary banknote of the
     "people's money," featuring Tiananmen Gate.

"No more arresting emblems of the modern culture of nationalism exist than cenotaphs and tombs of Unknown Soldiers," says Benedict Anderson.[16] The Monument to the People's Heroes captures the way in which a culture of Chinese nationalism has been built upon a bedrock that both calls forth a sacrifice for nation and stirs the heart to show that one's cause is true.

Cenotaphs and tombs invoke "ghostly *national* imaginings," but they also lead to silent introspective prayer.[17] The Monument to the People's Heroes, however, invokes a sense of liberation through struggle and transforms these imaginings into a politicized incitement to remember. The crowd is called upon to remember that collectively it is they, the masses, who make history. The monument reflects this conception. Despite the fact that each panel was sculpted by a different artist, every face shows the same steely determination, every pose flags a similar revolutionary gesture, and every struggle is a struggle forward. The cumulative effect is immensely powerful. In this way, the specific mass-based history of Chinese liberation becomes another confirmation of Marx's famous dictum that "the history of all hitherto existing society is the history of class struggles."[18]

By the time the monument was unveiled, however, struggle had given way to construction. Beijing was being renovated, and Tiananmen Square itself had become a major construction site.

Renovation of the square began at the very height of enthusiasm for the ultimately disastrous Great Leap Forward, in 1958. The redesign of the square was part of a major redevelopment of the city that involved the construction of what were called the Ten Great Projects. Like the Great Leap itself, this major drive was designed to show the ability of humans to act in superhuman fashion when inspired by an intense and personal commitment to politics. The result was astonishing. In just ten months all but one of the major projects were completed in what could well be described

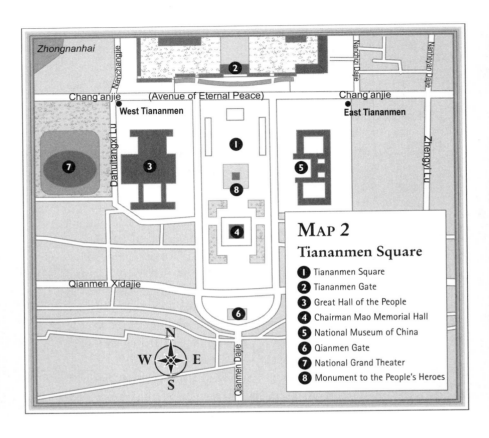

Zhongnanhai

Chang'anjie (Avenue of Eternal Peace)

West Tiananmen

East Tiananmen

Chang'anjie

Qianmen Xidajie

MAP 2
Tiananmen Square

1. Tiananmen Square
2. Tiananmen Gate
3. Great Hall of the People
4. Chairman Mao Memorial Hall
5. National Museum of China
6. Qianmen Gate
7. National Grand Theater
8. Monument to the People's Heroes

7   The Monument to the People's Heroes.

as the first postrevolutionary building boom. As well as the renovation of the square, the construction projects included the Beijing Railway Station, the Cultural Palace of Nationalities, the National Minorities Hotel, the Military Museum, the National Agricultural Exhibition Center, the State Guest House, and the Overseas Chinese Hotel.[19] Easily the most spectacular of all the renovations were those associated with the new and grandiose Tiananmen Square.

Mao had demanded a square "big enough to hold an assembly of one billion," and, at just under half a million square meters, Tiananmen Square came pretty close.[20] The Chinese Communists had created the largest urban open-air public space in the world. In a James Joycean "here comes everybody" kind of revolutionary moment, millions of Red Guards descended upon Tiananmen Square in August 1966 to parade before Chairman Mao at the beginning of the Cultural Revolution and watch as the Chairman himself donned the Red Guard armband.

Built to accommodate these revolutionary tourists, even Tiananmen began to sink under its own weight. Architects and engineers discovered damage and distortion in Tiananmen Gate in the early 1960s. Plans for repair were ready by 1965, but the Cultural Revolution delayed implementation until 1969.[21] The engineers had concluded that little could be done to prop up the ailing 550-year-old structure, but its political importance precluded demolition. The solution was a bizarre plan to replicate the entire original structure in secret brick by brick and tile by tile on the original site. Thus, long before economic reform made piracy commonplace, Maoism introduced the concept to New China.

In other words, Tiananmen Gate, that potent political symbol where Mao stood and proclaimed New China and where his picture still hangs today, is a fake. The secrecy surrounding its construction stands in sharp contrast to the publicity and fanfare attending the rebuilding of the square during the Great Leap.

After enlargement, the building work redefining the perimeter of the square began in earnest. On the western side arose the parliament building known as the Great Hall of the People, on the east the Revolutionary Museum (now renamed the National Museum of China). With these renovations, Tiananmen displaced the Forbidden City as the unquestionable center of Beijing.

Before liberation, of course, it had all been very different. For much of the later dynastic period, the Forbidden City (or Imperial Palace, as it is sometimes known) had been the symbolic heart of Beijing. According to legend, that centrality had a divine origin. It is said that when the Ming emperor Zhudi proposed to move the capital to Beijing, he ran into opposition from the Ministry of Construction. The records of the ministry showed that on the site of the proposed new capital there had once been an ocean called the Youzhou Sea of Misery *(kuhai youzhou),* which was home to an evil water dragon. The omens indicated that this dragon must be expelled before the capital could be built.

Two generals with skills in exorcism volunteered for the task. As both were ambitious, they decided to separate for ten days and work out their own individual plans. One would go to the east of Beijing, the other to the west, returning to an agreed-upon spot to compare notes. As each went on his separate way, something strange started happening. No matter where each went, a child with a red shirt would appear and advise him to "draw things according to me. Then everything will be fine."[22] On the fifth day the child appeared again, this time dressed in a lotus-leaf cape. The red ribbons that tied the cape to the shoulders of the child waved in the air like arms in the wind. Only then did both generals independently realize that they had had a visitation from the legendary "Eight-arm Nezha."[23] When they reunited and compared their plans for the city, they found that they were identical. The Eight-Arm Nezha had given them both a city plan modeled on his own eight-armed bodily form. Each of the eight outstretched arms of the child

8   Three panels on the Monument to the People's Heroes,

portraying Mao's vision of modern Chinese history.

spirit formed the west-east axis of the city. The main south-north axis, formed by Nezha's trunk, became Beijing's main axis. This city plan, in other words, followed a logic not unlike that of the T-O maps of ancient Christendom, which rendered the crucified body of Christ as various points of the compass, with Jerusalem at—and as—its heart. In the case of Beijing, the Forbidden City became the mystical center of imperial power, and the home of the emperor.

A similar design was offered in a more prosaic but no less venerated form in the pages of that most sacred of ancient Chinese books, the *Zhouli*: "Inside a walled compound there is a straight road. There is one that will run from south to north, but there will be nine that run from West to East." Apart from adding a ninth west-east arm, the *Zhouli* plan offered a clearer sense of the spiritual significance of the Imperial Palace: "At the centre of this walled city is the palace of the emperor. On the left perimeter of the palace there is the *Tai Miao*—the altar to the ancients and the gods. This is where the emperor's ancestral records are held. On the right hand side is the *Shejitan* or the altar to the earth and harvest gods, and this is where the emperor will pray to the gods of the earth and harvest."[24] Part church, part government office, part imperial home, the palace had both pragmatic and sacred cosmological significance.

The spiritual significance is captured in the architecture itself. The palace of the Forbidden City is reputed to have 9,999 rooms—in terms of Chinese numerology, just one room short of perfection. Perfection came in the form of the mythic Jade Emperor, who lived in heaven, and who was said to have had a 10,000-room palace. The earthly emperor, as the son of heaven, could not presume to rival or surpass the father.[25] Yet the palace was also the place of more earthly concerns.

The interior design of the Forbidden City reflected this complex of the lofty and the mundane. The palace closest to the main, southern entrance was where the business of state was conducted while the northern rear of the palace was reserved for businesses and markets. In traditional China, dealing with matters of state was a noble occupation, but mercantilism was not.

After the Communist victory in 1949 this cosmological order was shaken. The recentering of the city at Tiananmen Square effectively made the old Imperial Palace the northern "backyard."

That the Communist Party imposed its own cosmology upon the city is confirmed by one of the chief architects of the 1950s Tiananmen construction project, Chen Gan. In Chen's view, the Taoist metaphysical cosmology of geomancy was giving way to a new, scientific framework embodying the principles of reasoning drawn from Friedrich Engels' *Dialectics of Nature*. Starting from Engels' observations about the importance of the number zero, Chen explains how Tiananmen became a crucial point in this new cosmology.

Building on Hegel's assertion that "the nothing of a something is a *determinate* nothing," Engels made this "determinate nothing" the key point of spatial measurement. For Engels, zero was of greater import than any negative or positive number insofar as it was the point on a line upon which all other points become dependent. The spatial representation of zero became the site of the Monument to the People's Heroes; the monument and the square surrounding it formed the Archimedean fulcrum of political leverage, and it was made that way by the building of the so-called Ten Major Projects. Collectively, these projects eliminated the old, cosmologically inspired south-north axis. The new central axis ran from the west to the east along the Avenue of Eternal Peace and was dominated by the Ten Great Projects *(Shi da jianzhu)* of the Great Leap Forward. Tiananmen was at the heart of the new grid. With Mao's oversized portrait hanging over Tiananmen Gate to the north, the Great Hall of the People flanking the square to the west, and the equally spectacular Revolutionary Museum (now the National Museum) on the east, the symbolism of the square was complete. Mao (his portrait), the people (or their representatives in the Great Hall), and their collective revolutionary memories (in the museum) formed the built environment that dominated the square. Yet despite the very new manifest meaning it held, Tiananmen, still rather paradoxically, reinforced a latent and quite traditional form of symbolic logic. Ultimately, it produced a space that could only be understood as a mimetic reconfiguration of the architectonics of the traditional compound house, the *siheyuan*.

Like the Imperial Palace, the traditional compound house was surrounded on all four sides by walls, but within those walls the spatial arrangements were of great symbolic importance. The main rooms, at the northern end of the household, were designated as the parental apartments and were known as the *zhengfang* or *beifang*. These apartments normally consisted of three rooms: the *dongxiang,* on the northeastern corner; the *xixiang,* on the northwestern corner; and the *tangwu,* in the center. If the *tangwu* was not used to house the ancestral tablets it would be used as the parental room; then the eldest brother would live in the *dongxiang* and the second eldest in the *xixiang.* The southern wing was always reserved for animals or servants. At the center of the whole compound was an open courtyard, known as the *tianjing,* or well of heaven, where the whole family—ideally four generations— congregated.

In Tiananmen Square we discover a similar architectonic structure, but one that reinforces the message of socialism. The building to the north of the square is Tiananmen Gate, where Mao proclaimed the founding of the People's Republic and where his large portrait still hangs. This became the new *tangwu.* To the west, the *dongxiang* was transformed into the Great Hall of the People, while to the east the Revolutionary Museum became a metaphorical *xixiang.* The square itself, the *people's* square, with the Monument to the People's Heroes at its heart, became the *tianjing,* or heavenly well, to which the people's memories would be tied and from which the revolution would draw its strength. The result was a structure giving protean life to a socialist imaginary.

The square confirms the legacy of revolution; it highlights where the people have been (the museum), how they will unite and go forward (the Great Hall of the People), and how their aims will be advanced (through the thought of Mao Zedong, captured in the portrait on Tiananmen Gate). From 1977, the configuration of the square would also, rather bizarrely, flag the slow decay of this particular dream of socialism and the rise of a very different vision of China's future.

On 9 September 1976 Mao Zedong finally went to "meet Marx," as the Chinese Communists euphemistically say. A crisis in the leadership followed, as no one had dared speak of funeral arrangements while Mao remained alive. Mao had specified that his body be cremated, but the Party leadership initially decided on a fifteen-day period of mourning during which Mao's temporarily preserved body would be displayed in the Great Hall of the People. Doctors were called in to ensure short-term preservation of the corpse.[26]

The next day, however, the Central Committee changed its mind and decided to preserve Mao's body in perpetuity. Thus, when the period of mourning came to an end, the corpse was whisked off to a clinic within the 305 military hospital, and work began on devising a means to ensure a permanently preserved corpse. Code-named "the 769 project," the effort met with difficulties not least because of the initial indecision about what to do with the corpse, resulting in significant delays in its treatment. This factor, combined with a lack of expertise in the art of bodily preservation and a series of technical errors during the actual embalming process, led to real fears that the body was beyond repair. According to one of Mao's doctors, Li Zhisui, who authored a controversial account of the period, a team of researchers was secretly dispatched to England to investigate how Madame Tussaud's Wax Museum made its effigies.[27] The result, he claims, was the production of two Maos:

one made of wax, the other a mixture of Mao body parts and assorted chemicals. Both would be stored in the mausoleum, and when repairs were needed on the corpse, the wax dummy would be put on display.

While medical researchers continued to struggle to preserve the decaying corpse and others worked on the wax effigy, architects rushed to design a fitting mausoleum for what they hoped would be the preserved corpse of their beloved Chairman. By this stage the Party leadership had decided that the Chairman Mao Memorial Hall would be built on the southern side of Tiananmen Square and would have, as its centerpiece, a crystal sarcophagus in which the corpse of Mao would be permanently on display. Thus, while the portrait of Mao would sit at the northern end of the square, the decaying body of the Chairman was to be put on permanent display at the southern end. This siting of the mausoleum destroyed any lingering connection between socialism and the metaphors of traditional cosmology.

Perhaps such total destruction of the old cosmology was thought necessary in order to institute a new, socialist one? After all, had Stalin, in offering his eulogy to Lenin before the latter was embalmed, not spoken of Communists' being made of "special stuff"? Had this statement not in turn suggested, as Katherine Verdery comments, that "the communist body does not decay!"? Verdery goes further, suggesting that the mummification of Lenin, in offering the possibility of everlasting life, is perhaps "the greatest communist." Verdery is not alone in drawing on such thoughts to understand the political lives of dead bodies. Vladislav Todorov argues that Lenin's embalmed body was "a titanic will to power." "Like a marvelous pupa," he speculates, "Lenin will take off some day from his own mummy." His "perennial body" becomes a sign of the "omni-here-present" of Party power, and his mausoleum is like a "marvelous catapult constructed to launch Lenin back into the living world."[28] Perhaps the idea of embalming was the Communist way of cheating time itself by offering the possibility of everlasting life. If so, the Chinese Communists had insufficiently attended to their own ancient cosmology. Far from flagging eternal life, the construction of the Chairman Mao Memorial Hall totally blocked the south-north flow of *qi* and, perhaps more than anything else, came to signal the death of Mao's version of socialism.

From his sarcophagus, Mao would witness the wholesale transformation of his city and the rapid decay of his socialist dream. The once highly charged political symbols of his rule, the Mao badges, the Little Red Books, the posters and busts of his image, were now mere market curiosities or trinkets of a new consumer fad. The city that had been at the heart of his revolutionary dream was being transformed into a hub of global capital. His decaying body would oversee his own demise. Mao's time has come and gone; his politically centered world is now a distant memory. A new and vibrant Beijing has emerged with very different dreams of the future. Let us map these new dreams by looking more closely at the ways they have remapped this city.

2   THE MAP

"We have not attended adequately to the ways in which states are spatialized," write James Ferguson and Akhil Gupta.[1] Let us try to rectify this omission by looking at the state's redeployment of space in just one city, the city of Beijing. The Planning Exhibition Hall is the only place where it is possible to look down on the city and grasp it in its entirety. There is a certain pleasure in this experience. It is a pleasure captured in the words of Michel de Certeau as he gazed down from the 110th floor of New York City's World Trade Center in 1998: "It's hard to be down, when you are up."[2] There is, however, another factor, one suggesting something less innocent in this particular pleasure. There is something about the overview that speaks to the questions of how the state sees and how it spatially rearranges a city's landscape.

Timothy Mitchell acknowledged these questions in passing when he spoke of the cravings of colonialism for the overview. To have a distance from a place in order to "picture a place" was a sentiment felt by Western nineteenth-century "gentlemen" of all persuasions, whether romantics or hard-nosed pragmatists, writers or scientists. The "point of view" was as much a craving for writers as it was for daguerreotypists who required an overarching vista.[3] It was, in many ways, part of a will to power; a desire to see in order to grasp, to control . . . to colonize.

At least until the modern era, the overview, the panorama, the overarching perspective were restricted to birds and gods. Modern technology has changed all that. Now we can look down from lofty buildings, and yet our feet never have to leave the ground. Looking down upon Beijing from the air-conditioned comfort of the Planning Exhibition Hall yields just such a view. From here, the city is a sleeping beauty, even when it is wide awake. No traffic snarls, no blustery winds, no pushy crowds or any of the other small irritants that encumber life and bend and complicate a city into something other than pure vista. The viewing platform of Beijing's Planning Exhibition Hall offers us the perfect overview, one that appears too

9 An overview of Beijing.

beautiful, too magical, and too good to be true. In this case, it simply is too good to be true.

Beijing's Planning Exhibition Hall, you see, is not the Chinese equivalent of New York City's Empire State Building, the Petronas Towers of Kuala Lumpur, or the Eiffel Tower of Paris. It is a moderate-sized modern five-story inner-city office block just off Tiananmen Square in Qianmen whose entire fourth floor has been converted into an observation deck overlooking a massive scale model of the city of Beijing laid out on the floor below. Covering the whole of the 1,300-square-meter surface, this scaled-down replica shows every street, every building, every monument, every park, every road, every thing, in miniaturized detail.

No other place in Beijing affords such an "authentic" overview. Even if there were buildings tall enough, the smog and sprawl of this city would deprive us of an opportunity. Too many people needing too many apartments have resulted in too much sprawl. Too many cars and too much industry have created a world of too many anxieties and too much pollution. Only at the Planning Exhibition Hall can we see the sprawl scaled down to manageable size in a smog-free environment.

Viewing the city in its entirety and in all its clarity allows the symbolic aspects to shine through, and in a highly political place like Beijing, what shines brightest is state power. "The metaphors through which states are imagined are important," Ferguson and Gupta rightly observe.[4] But the metaphors of power that have shaped Beijing's built environment are best seen by a close examination of the replica model at the Planning Exhibition Hall. Here, the metaphors of state are not about individual buildings but about their collective effect on the framing of the city as a whole. Part map, part history, part archeology, this overview charts the lines of power that flow through Beijing.

Tracing the line of buildings—from the Temple of Heaven to the Drum and Bell Towers—along the south-north axis brings into

10   Replica Beijing.

focus the faint traces of the ancient dynastic city. Now shift attention to the numerous Western-style, turn-of-the-twentieth-century buildings in the very heart of the city—from the British-built Eastern Zhengyangmen Railway Station to the French wing of the Beijing Hotel—and see how Western imperialism tried to impose its own form of orthodoxy upon this Eastern city. Then turn to the central west-east axis, the Avenue of Eternal Peace, with the Ten Great Projects of the Mao era peppering the route, to see how these landmarks reoriented the old dynastic axis of power. Last, look at Qianmen and behold the booming city of today's economic reform.

Outside the Planning Exhibition Hall, down on the streets of Qianmen, there is movement everywhere. Even the ground moves beneath our feet as the machinery of economic reform tears down neighborhoods and redefines others. This revolution has spread beyond the inner city, transforming once-sleepy outer suburbs like Zhongguancun into glittering commercial high-tech hubs. Six ring roads and many feeder highways have produced an urban jungle choked with cars, snaking their way through the forests of highrises. New suburbs are being built while old ones disappear. The whole city has exploded upward and outward. This booming economy now marks the face of Beijing in a way that almost eclipses the dynastic, imperialist, and political pasts. This city exudes confidence, and that confidence is best expressed by Beijing's new showcase architecture. The land of the economic miracle now boasts buildings that flag the miraculous. They are big, bold, and out of this world. The Central China Television (CCTV) Headquarters and Cultural Center building covers an area the size of thirty-seven football fields.[5] It rises 230 meters from one column, then swings wildly to join another column, forming a unique angular shape. Spectacular new venues such as the National Stadium and National Aquatic Center reconfigure the city skyline and give meaning to the government slogan "New Beijing, New Olympics."

Meanwhile, on the showcase Avenue of Eternal Peace, a space-

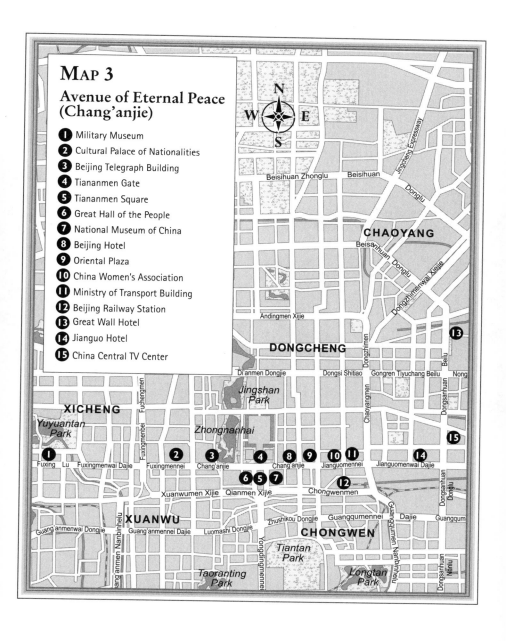

MAP 3
Avenue of Eternal Peace (Chang'anjie)

1. Military Museum
2. Cultural Palace of Nationalities
3. Beijing Telegraph Building
4. Tiananmen Gate
5. Tiananmen Square
6. Great Hall of the People
7. National Museum of China
8. Beijing Hotel
9. Oriental Plaza
10. China Women's Association
11. Ministry of Transport Building
12. Beijing Railway Station
13. Great Wall Hotel
14. Jianguo Hotel
15. China Central TV Center

11   The Avenue of Eternal Peace.

ship has landed. Resembling something straight out of *Mars Attacks!*, it is parked right next to the greatest symbol of socialist political power in China, Tiananmen Square. This spaceship is called the National Grand Theater. "We come in peace," say the Martians of the movie before blasting everything around them to smithereens. This building, just by its very presence, is one big blast at the political past. Sitting in radical juxtaposition with the staid, old, formal political architecture of Tiananmen Square, the National Grand Theater compels us to turn our gaze from the old Beijing to the new.

The expressions of economic reform weren't always this confident. The architecture of the early years of economic reform displayed a penchant for verticality that was mixed not with confidence but rather with an odd anxiety born of questions of national identity. Once again, the showcase Avenue of Eternal Peace is the best place to register this uncertainty. Here the central government introduced and enforced a strict set of building codes that essentially demanded that any proposed building pay due attention to questions of utility, modernity, and Chineseness. The results were skyscrapers in fancy dress. Some were covered with a pastiche of garish red-lacquer ornamental columns, while more modernist efforts were simply "capped" with the overly ornate traditional Chinese-style green glazed roof.[6]

By the twenty-first century this stylistic uncertainty was gone; bold, new, and uncompromising structures bristling with confidence started to reshape Beijing's skyline. In many ways they are a parody of the state's demand for utility, modernity, and "Chineseness." If these buildings are indeed the flagships of a new design revolution that helps supply this city with new badges of identity, then the message seems to have been lost on the city street. Here colloquialism rips away at the designers' pretensions and collectively helps them to remap the main city thoroughfare in a way that owes allegiance to no master. For local residents, the National

Stadium is the "bird's nest" (niaochao), the National Aquatic Center the "water cube" (shuilifang), and the very controversial National Grand Theater the "huge egg" (judan). Lay disputes about the worth of any particular building have given rise to contending colloquialisms; the National Grand Theater, for example, has sometimes been described as a "broken shell surrounded by eggwhite" (liule danqing de danke), but it is just as likely to be called "a boiled egg floating in the water" (shuizhengdan). Although the building's French architect, Paul Andreu, has described his design as "a new district [sic] of spectacles and dreams open to one and all," the wild north winds that have always howled through the city envelop this gleaming silver shell in dust. The result is that the structure looks less like a source of dreams than a pile of shit—and that, apparently, is exactly how some wags refer to it.[7] Earlier architectural efforts from the 1980s and 1990s were not exempt from such street-level criticism. The Customs Building with its enormous archway opening was called "the trousers with its zipper down" until modesty and the wind-tunnel effect forced architects to redesign the structure. That ubiquitous flag of Chineseness, the green-tiled pagoda-style roof, is another form that leads to parody. Whereas in the past these "hats" sat above modest low-rise structures as they had done in ancient times, they now cap massive modernist skyscrapers. A powerful upward-thrusting object wearing a "green hat" may not mean much to a Westerner, but to a Chinese its meaning is obvious. The upward thrust, of course, suggests something very male, and the reference to "green hats," in Chinese slang, means to be cuckolded. Farther along the Avenue of Eternal Peace, the circular "belly" of the China Women's Association building suggests it has fallen pregnant, and the culprit, it is said, is its very manly neighbor, the red-capped Grand Temple, or, as it is officially known, the Ministry of Transport Building.

Such redescriptions of the built environment along the Avenue of Eternal Peace may appear absurd, vulgar, and whimsical, yet in

12   The Customs Building.

13   The China Women's Association building.

14   The red-capped Ministry of Transport Building.

a very Chinese way they are examples of what Mikhail Bakhtin might have called "grotesque realism"—that is, the absurdist, carnivalesque "turning of the tables" on the good-taste aesthetic realism of the ruling elite. Bodily references abound in such descriptions, and they invariably point to things that are literally below the belt; absurd names and slogans mimic and parody the upbeat Party slogans to unmask governmental pretensions and pretentiousness. Above all, and underpinning everything, as Bakhtin observed, there is laughter.

It is baroque laughter, laughter of the grotesque, laughter at the expense of power. Out of this laughter emerges an uncanny picture of the city. It presents a very different image of "the people" from the one encountered in propaganda posters. It is certainly not "the people" according to Mao; it is not "the people" who built his Avenue of Eternal Peace into a monument of socialism. Looking at their faces, their clothes, their way of walking, and, of course, the way they disparage the "official" built environment, we arrive at the same conclusion that André Breton did about the French working class: "No, it is not yet these who would be ready to create the Revolution."[8] Nevertheless, these are the people whose industry enabled the city's modernization and added more than forty-three kilometers to the Avenue of Eternal Peace, "modernizing" it beyond recognition. Over the 1990s they constructed twenty-one massive new building complexes along this thoroughfare, more than in the whole previous forty years of Maoist development. The result was that Mao's showpiece was a showpiece of Maoism no more. Indeed, it had become almost a critique of that era. No longer an exhibition space for Communist iconography, the newly enlarged avenue would even boast its own "Manhattan" in the form of a skyscraper street-scape called the "Wall Street" district. Farther toward the center of town, the avenue became the home of capitalist consumerism with the completion of the 880,000-square-meter shopping mall called the Oriental Plaza. And, of course, where would the avenue be without some signs of the state, represented here in myriad tall office blocks covering much of its south-central reach.

An avenue that was once a showpiece of socialism now sparkles in an altogether different register. All this is somewhat paradoxical, since it is based on the continued official socialist state's sponsorship of the cash register. As it rings out around the city, it sets off housing and apartment booms, transforming even the most backward and dilapidated of outlying suburbs into modern high-rise jungles. Just how far this boom has traveled along the road of modernization can be gauged by the ever-expanding system of ring roads around Beijing's ever-expanding girth. Here is a city of the new, the advanced, and the ultramodern demanding to be recognized as a global player.

These stupendous changes amount to a remapping of the imagination of both the city and the state. The built environment helps to make concrete the way the state "thinks" about things. The dynastic city, the Maoist city, and the city of economic reform all offer spatial maps of very different modes of government and of power in very different times. Yet it is only when we combine this overview with a more detailed interrogation of the projects and politics of these times that this becomes clear. So let us start to take a closer look . . .

Panning out from the Haussmann-like expanse of the inner city, across the wide, open boulevard called the Avenue of Eternal Peace, across an endless array of gray-tiled roofs that mark out the inner-city "conservation zones," and past 1960s-style apartments that once made up key components of the work-unit system, we repeatedly hit, as one hits speed bumps, Beijing's six concentric ring roads. The farther out we move, the clearer these concentric circles become as the rows of high-rise apartment buildings flanking the ring roads become lower and less tightly packed. Overall, they offer up a newer and much more vertical vision of the city.

15   The Third Ring Road.

To a Westerner, the visual statement being made may seem a perverse postmodern, dystopic parody of the comfortable tree-lined street of the bourgeoisie. It might appear as a confession carved into the landscape. Here is a city that speaks of socialism, but only under the rubric of development at all costs. For Chinese, however, an altogether different link might come to mind and lead to an altogether different appreciation of these developments. For Chinese, the ring roads look less like a perverse caricature of a comfortable bourgeois street than successive reworkings of the old city wall. These roads have become the architectural embodiment of a changed theatrical understanding of the city: five halos, five signs of modernity, five new city walls.

If the extension and refashioning of the Avenue of Eternal Peace tell us how economic reform has changed the metaphor of state in the inner city, the ring roads tell us something else. The first—which was rather perversely called the second ring road—was, to some degree, a legacy of the Maoist past. Construction of the second ring road and of the subway under it began in the early 1970s under the rule of Mao Zedong, but engineering problems hampered progress. By the time of their completion in the early 1980s, Mao was gone, and economic reform had been in place under Deng Xiaoping for more than three years. Thus economic reform seemed to show that it could deliver on things Maoism had failed to. Spanning two political eras, the decisions to start the project and to see it through to completion implicated both the Mao and Deng regimes in the demolition of the city wall. There is little of the old wall left now, and it is mainly in the names of suburbs that this old part of Beijing is memorialized. The one exception is Deshengmen.

Deshengmen, or Virtue and Victory Gate, is one of Beijing's many public transport hubs. It is also the name of the gate that stands at the heart of that hub. This gate was saved because Deshengmen was to dynastic China what the Arc de Triomphe was and still is to France. It was through this passageway that the con-

16   Deshengmen Gate now sits at the center of a huge spaghetti junction.

quering armies of the dynastic era traveled. So this gateway entrance was of particular significance and beauty. It was, therefore, saved, but only in a fashion.

Deshengmen Gate now forms the centerpoint of a huge spaghetti junction. It stands in the middle of a huge complex of roads on one edge of which is a major bus depot and on another a subway station. In such a setting this beautiful structure stands as a metaphor for tradition fenced in by modernity. All the other old gateway suburbs of the city wall have become mere subway-station and bus-stop names along the busy commuter route of the second ring road. It is at this point that, as de Certeau would put it, perspectival vision gives rise to prospective thinking.

The turbo-charged rate of change over the last few years has brought in its wake a transformation of the urban landscape. It has colonized the old Maoist view of modernity and turned it into a view of its own. If the Avenue of Eternal Peace shows us its power to transform Maoism into its opposite, the ring roads show us its power to colonize through expansion. Dynastic Beijing had three city walls, including the one surrounding the Forbidden City. Now there are in effect five city walls, taking the form of ring roads flanked by high-rises, extending concentrically outward from the path of the outermost old city wall. The dynastic city was fortified and inward looking. The ring roads have established a new, open, and ever-expansive metaphor of the state, one built upon economic instead of military might.

Power, it seems, no longer grows out of the barrel of a gun but comes through property investment. As the old fortifications and parapets gave way to the modern-day equivalent of the plowshare, the high-rise apartment block, a new metaphorics of modernity replaced the inward-looking military-based power of the dynastic era. Economic reform shared this vision of modernity with Maoism. Unlike Maoism, however, economic reform delivered on its promises of total transformation. Where Maoism tried to modernize the state through mobilization of people's power and failed, economic reform has used more conventional and materialist methods and succeeded beyond all expectations.

Maoist modernity pursued development via politics and deliberately set out to replace the symbols of the old with those of the socialist new. The political campaigns against the "Four Olds"—old customs, old cultures, old habits, and old ideas—clearly had an architectural dimension. The attempt to replace the old city wall with those ultimate signs of modernity, subways and highways, was a powerful statement. But so too was the statement that socialism was overthrowing the old dynastic order by overthrowing the classic longitudinal axis with a new latitudinal strip running along the Avenue of Eternal Peace. This was a statement both about socialism and, perhaps more surprisingly, about modernity. If the work method of this project spoke of Maoism (although the building style was Soviet), then the idea underpinning the spinning of this axis, we might venture to say, was both political *and* scientistic. Why scientistic?

The early history of Western architecture teaches us that the longitudinal plan was central to the construction of early European churches, for it instituted an architectural flow that would lead the worshipper all the way to the altar. The centralized floor plan that treated longitude and latitude equally was viewed with great suspicion and even open hostility. Over time, however, the centralized plan became a crucial component of both church architecture and city planning in the West. Thenceforth the combination of longitude and latitude would be a key element in any discussion of the organization of space.[9]

Perhaps it is going too far to suggest that it was the church's penchant for focusing exclusively on the longitudinal that led Soviet advisers to cleave toward a latitudinal axis in reconstructing a new and socialist Beijing. Be that as it may, for Chinese Communists this shift was a clear shot at the south-north symbolism of ancient Chinese power. Perhaps both Soviet and Chinese regarded this plan as a crucial "modern" weapon in their struggle against the old society and old thinking, although they did so in different ways and for different reasons.

Whatever the motives behind the decision, one thing is clear: the latitudinal plan took tangible form during the 1950s with the Ten Major Projects and decisively displaced the old, longitudinal city axis. This socialist undertaking was clearly more than a city plan. It was a plan of attack. It was part of a struggle against an old cosmology, manifested in built form, that socialism promised to overcome.

Heaven is round, and earth is square; west is *yin* and east is *yang*; the masses wore gray and the emperor gold—or so the old cosmological ordering of the city would have had it. The hexagram, or *bagua*, of the sacred book of divination, the *I Ching* (*Yijing*; Book of Changes), formed the perfect structural guide not just for the city plan but also for life itself. Whether it was about bodily health or the good ordering of households on the basis of *fengshui*, it was always about *qi*, or the flow of spirit.

Every house, temple, and government building in the ancient city was ordered in such a way that it would guide *qi* in a manner that ensured the correct balance of spiritual forces. The plan was designed to tip these forces of the spirit in favor of harmony and prosperity, and to do this it relied upon ancient Taoist philosophy. The ideal flow of spirit would occur via a south-north axis running through the center of the city. This axis would link the circular dome of the Temple of Heaven in the south to the square compound module at the center of imperial power, the Forbidden City. From this heart of earthly power, the axis would strike north until it reached the Bell and Drum Towers. These would regulate the *qi* by regulating time. The axis would run through all nine inner-city gates, and because the gates would remain open in the daylight hours, no part of this built environment would ever interrupt the spirit that flowed auspiciously through the city.

This *qi* was the lifeblood not just of the city but also of the entire Celestial Empire. Running through a series of city gates until finally flowing in and then out of the earthly square of the Forbidden City, this south-north axis regulated the world of the living. Yet the flow of spirit was itself regulated by the opening and closing of the city gates, and those operations were, in turn, ordered around a set of routines enforced by the Bell and Drum Towers. Thus the two towers were a pair of cogs in a cosmic wheel designed to bring forth stability and harmony not just to the city of Beijing or even China, but to the whole of heaven and earth. Hence the towers would fit into a city plan that was, in fact, much more than an urban design. Indeed, to read this city plan as merely a plan is to seriously underestimate its cosmic significance. The flow of *qi* was central to this project, and the regulation of it was crucial to the city's sense of power and stability.

Hence, when the bells rang out from one tower to announce the dawning of a new day and the opening of the city gates, while at dusk the drumbeat from the other tower reverberated across the city to signal the closing of the city gates and the end of another day, they were doing more than marking time. Between the morning chimes and evening drums, the Drum Tower issued a beat every two hours, establishing the rhythm of everyday life in the streets of Beijing.

This mode of marking time came abruptly and violently to an end at the turn of the twentieth century when the Eight-Power Allied Forces of imperialism sacked the city and bayoneted the skins of the imperial drums.[10]

Within a year, chimes from a Western clock would replace the bells and drums of the two towers. They would boom out from the clock tower on the British-built Eastern Zhengyangmen Railway Station. Constructed in 1901, it was just a stone's throw to the

17   The bayoneted skins of the imperial drums.

south of Tiananmen Square. This classic Victorian-era railway station with its gigantic clock tower cast a shadow over the whole of central Beijing, but it cast an even larger shadow over the imperial order. In this respect, the railway station was a profound and aggressive statement of imperialist intent.

Suggesting that the power of Western imperialism lay not just in the naked exertion of military power but, more profoundly, in its ability to control the world of time and space through science and technology, the building of a railway station constituted a profoundly modernist colonial statement. The railway line, after all, was the first "road" adapted entirely to the demands of the machine age. Indeed, this technology made track and train inseparable. With the railways, says Wolfgang Schivelbusch, "mechanical regularity triumphed over natural irregularity," leading to a speeding up of time and a need for regularity in its keeping.[11] In other words, the railway and its station required the clock to make sense of speed and time.[12] The clock tower was a profoundly new way of controlling time, measuring it and enforcing the will of an alien temporality upon the city. Later this building would be joined by other Western institutions, such as banks and hotels, which would crowd into the central city area and, like the railway station, require the delivery of time in this particular way. Beijing would thus be disciplined and partly transformed by the "culture" of these new building works.

As the initial sign of this impending invasion, the Eastern Zhengyangmen Railway Station was perhaps the most significant and certainly the most intrusive of all these Western symbols of dominance. It would openly flout the ancient cosmology by ignoring concerns about the south-north flow of spirit; the height of its clock tower manifested a disregard of imperial edicts prohibiting any structure taller than the Imperial Palace; and, of course, the hourly chimes from the clock tower displaced the gongs and drumbeats of ancient Beijing time. Even when the skins on the imperial

18   The British-built Eastern Zhengyangmen Railway Station.

drums were replaced and the beat and gong of drums and bells rang out once more, the battle over time and the cosmology that underpinned it had already been lost. The forces of the old Celestial Empire would struggle on, ringing their bells and banging their drums for another twenty-three years, but when the last emperor, Pu Yi, was finally forced from the Imperial Palace, never to return, these sounds were heard no more. Today only a memory of that radically different temporality lives on. It is captured in the expression *chenzhong mugu*—the morning bell and the evening drum—which even now reminds every Chinese of an ancient world of understanding that once emanated from these twin towers.

Even before they fell silent, in the interval when they had been robbed of their mystical meaning yet still kept sending out their ancient sounds, they began to play a key role in a wholly new set of concerns: nationalism. As the site where the "crimes of the foreign devils" were plain for all to see, the damaged skins of the Drum Tower would become a national rallying point throughout the early years of the twentieth century.[13] Yet even during these moments of resistance, when nationalists rallied in protest at the foot of the Drum Tower, they were setting their watches to the time that rang out from the Western clock tower to the south rather than to the beat of the ancient drums above them. And when liberation finally came, it used these same Western hands to turn time and set a course for modernization. In postliberation China, that moment came with the building of the Beijing Telegraph Building.

The first major new building project of the revolution and one of the key projects of the first five-year economic plan, the Beijing Telegraph Building was constructed under the close supervision of the State Planning Commission. Sited on the west-east corridor of the Avenue of Eternal Peace, it rose seventy-three meters and stood for years as the tallest building in Beijing. Begun on 21 April 1956 and completed on 21 September 1958 at a cost of 9.8 million renminbi (1.2 million U.S. dollars), it was designed by the Western-

19   The Beijing Telegraph Building.

trained Chinese architect Lin Leyi (1916–1988) in a symmetrical, neoclassical style typical of all socialist built forms. Its centerpiece was a four-faced clock tower oriented to the four cardinal directions of the compass. The clock chimed every hour from six in the morning until ten at night.[14]

Yet this clock did not chime in the same way as other clocks. Whereas the British-built clock tower of the Eastern Zhengyangmen Railway Station noted the hour by a single chime, the Beijing Telegraph Building boomed out the first verse of the unofficial anthem of the revolution, "The East Is Red." On the hour every hour between six and ten, it spread the message of revolution. Luckily, it's a great tune!

Here, then, was the new Drum Tower of the revolution, China's very own socialist Big Ben. Like an update of the modernist message offered first by the Eastern Zhengyangmen Railway Station, the Beijing Telegraph Building linked time, speed, and technology. Whereas the imperialist turn-of-the-century imagination had run time down a set of railway tracks, by the mid-twentieth century wireless technology allowed time to take flight. Communications became the new harbinger of the modern, and the Beijing Telegraph Building not only signaled a new era in the pairing of telecommunications and time, but also enabled Mao to give the "gift" of time to the Chinese people. In effect, the tower liberated as well as updated the message of modernism.

In terms of style, location, and even the timing of its construction—not to mention the tune that rang out from its towers—the building was a statement of socialist modernity. In terms of both ancient tradition and imperialism, it had something to say. The Drum and Bell Towers had regulated the flow of qi along the dynastic south-north axis; the Telegraph Building was the first of a series of socialist constructions that displaced the old axis with a new, socialist corridor along the Avenue of Eternal Peace. The Eastern Zhengyangmen Railway Station had been built under imperialist duress; the Beijing Telegraph Building, it was claimed, was erected by "liberated workers" voluntarily expressing their newfound freedom through this work. Indeed, in these terms, the Telegraph Building is possibly the first major site of a new revolutionary work style in which enthusiasm would be harnessed and sent onto the building sites of socialism. This would become known as the Maoist mass line.

The rather orthodox socialist-realist design adopted by the architect Lin Leyi tends to mask the radical nature of the work ethic driving the construction. The Beijing Telegraph Building was a concrete expression of a wholly new way of being political. The project was not just building work; it was a way of globalizing the Communists' world by showing that even a building site "gives to things their look and to men their outlook," as Heidegger once remarked.[15] This construction work not only relied upon the idea of sacrifice; it also fostered it.

Sacrifice, as a form of giving beyond measure, was in many ways simply a new, materialist version of *qi,* the *qi* of the socialist state that, once harnessed, could foster "more, faster, better, and cheaper" *(duo kuai hao sheng)* production. Once they had been tested successfully during the construction of the Beijing Telegraph Building, both these work styles and this style of thought could be applied more generally. The building of the Beijing Telegraph Building was thus a harbinger of things to come. But how quickly they would come was something of a shock. Even before the workers had put the finishing touches on the Beijing Telegraph Building on 21 September 1958, a new and even more grandiose building project was being laid out. This epic expression of the revolution would be called the Ten Great Projects.

On 6 September 1958, as workers toiled to finish the Beijing Telegraph Building, more than 1,000 architects and urban planners were summoned to Beijing. They were told that to commemorate ten years of the socialist revolution, the Party planned to build ten

20   The Great Hall of the People.

21   The Revolutionary Museum (now the National Museum of China).

22   The Beijing Railway Station.

structures even bigger and more monumental than the Beijing Telegraph Building. The Party leadership then handed out a list of the buildings it wanted constructed by the crucial tenth-anniversary celebration, on 1 October 1959. Within ten days the architects and urban planners had submitted more than 100 design plans, and by the end of September a selection committee had chosen the winning designs.[16] If the design and selection process had been quick, the speed and scale of the construction work that followed were dazzling. In less than a year, the Great Hall of the People, the Revolutionary Museum, the Beijing Railway Station, the Minorities Exhibition Hall, and the Military Museum would go up along the new west-east corridor of the Avenue of Eternal Peace. Elsewhere in the city, specific sites were designated to host other great revolutionary monuments—the National Agricultural Exhibition Center in Chaoyangmen, the Beijing Workers' Stadium near Sanlitun. Some buildings would fade from the agenda as the euphoria of the Great Leap turned into the nightmare of the famine, but those that did get built would shine. Together the Ten Great Projects would leave the most visible mark of Beijing's political past upon the later urban landscape. They would not only shift the city axis and create a new cityscape; they would also show how a people, caught in a political maelstrom that promised a new way of life, could build a life for themselves based on sacrifice, heroics, and the gift of political commitment.

"Overtake Britain in seven years and the United States in fifteen" was one of the crucial catch cries of this period and this movement.[17] Using the same military strategy that had been applied during the war and was now being applied to construction work, the Great Leap Forward carried this ethos into the economy as a whole. Peasants and workers, inspired by Mao and the revolution, would work harder and in a more innovative way. Corners would be cut, new, often faulty, methods tested, and more chances taken in this new long march toward modernity. Throughout the campaign the metaphor of war loomed large, and nowhere more so than in the construction industry. As Wu Hung notes, the Ten Great Projects were built on the basis of the wartime military strategy.[18] Essentially, this meant that the same concentrated heroic spirit that had led the Communist guerrilla fighters to victory during the war of national liberation would now be applied to the socialist construction phase. Had the guerrilla war not been won despite the fact that the revolutionary soldiers had been forced to eat dried grain and fight with antiquated weapons? In contrast, had the enemy not had better food and superior weaponry? Yet still this enemy had lost to Mao's ragtag band of revolutionaries. They had lost because, unlike Mao's army, the enemy lacked the inspiration and political intensity that would drive the committed to fight not just for their lives but also for their cause. Political commitment was the key to their success, and now it became the means of overcoming any obstacle.

The Communist construction strategy emerged out of this sense of commitment, sacrifice, and politics. It was a politics of the heroic, of the sacrificial, of political intensity. If wars against mammon could lead to liberation, why couldn't that same mass-line power be set to work to liberate the people from nature? Time and a lack of machinery would not impede this socialist construction campaign. Indeed, hardships would spur the true revolutionary to even greater heroic feats. This was a life-and-death struggle in which, across the country, millions would die trying to achieve the impossible dream of the Great Leap Forward. In this context, we might think of the Ten Great Projects as monuments to those millions who lost their lives in the Great Leap folly. Yet to redescribe these projects only as monuments to the campaign dead seriously underestimates the passion and commitment that fueled the construction of these buildings. Indeed the passion and commitment the workers showed was, in many ways, the same sort of spirit that fueled the whole of the Great Leap project. The People's Daily, the Party newspaper, conveys a sense of that spirit.

Workers became midwives of revolution when the *People's Daily* claimed that the Ten Great Projects were the "Children of the Great Leap Forward." Far from being graveyard monuments to the needless loss of life during a massively failed project, the Ten Projects still stand, with slight unease, as monuments to Maoism's claim that a people fired by political commitment was ready to offer the ultimate sacrifice. It was this narrative that was carried in the *People's Daily* at the time: "These buildings are cast-iron proof of the Great Leap Forward and [our] high-speed development program. This is a record-breaking success story and a pinnacle in our architectural history."[19]

These days, a quiet discomfort persists about the story of the Ten Great Projects; by and large, it is a story repressed and buried by the story of the campaign dead. Nevertheless, the triumphalist story is worth retelling, for only in understanding it can we understand how an entire nation came to live through the notion of sacrifice and in doing so sacrifice so many of its own for the utopian cause. The Ten Great Projects featured all the same dynamics that inspired the Great Leap, but instead of leading to millions of deaths they led, at the very least, to a change in Beijing's skyline.

Hundreds of thousands of model workers were involved in the construction of the Ten Great Projects. They came from across China, in response to a summons to every province to identify and send its most productive construction workers. It became a matter of prestige to be selected to work. Model workers were lauded and sent off with much fanfare, political incentives were awarded for the most diligent, and thousands would volunteer to participate. For a while, this building project even changed the way people spoke.

The traditional standard opening greeting among Chinese, the familiar and habitualized "hello," was never really "How are you?" (*Ni hao ma?*)—that was a later transcription from the West—but rather "Have you eaten?" (*Ni chifanle ma?*). But for a short time in the late 1950s, the most popular greeting in Beijing became "Have you volunteered yet for work at the site of the Great Hall of the People?"[20] Enthusiasm, spontaneity, and a sense of the need for sacrifice were wedded to a sense of discipline, allowing Maoism to recruit from Bakhtin's festival of fools, transforming the masses first into revolutionary soldiers, then into revolutionary workers. Unlike Bakhtin's carnival, however, there would be no counternarrative of power, no burlesque jokes, no toilet humor. This would be a carnival of the mind that was wedded to the discipline of a Party project. As Party mindedness enveloped the nation, 20,000 people donned the uniform of construction workers and offered themselves as a sacrifice to help build a new world by constructing structures such as the Great Hall. It was in building the Ten Great Projects that we find the Party requiring more than laboring bodies; they required the workers' bodies, hearts, and souls.

Designed by the noted architect Zhang Bo, with assistance from Zhang Dongri, the floor space of the Great Hall spanned an incredible 170,000 square meters. Inside it would feature a 10,000-seat Great Hall and a banquet room said to be the size of a soccer field. One hundred forty thousand workers would labor, day and night, to complete the project in just ten months.[21] The extraordinary speed of construction is all the more astonishing given the limited resources available to these builders. Even basic machinery, such as cranes and other heavy lifting equipment, was rare. Like the guerrilla army with which the Communists had come to power, these soldiers of construction would learn to make do, to compromise, to be flexible, and ultimately to rely upon the strength of their own commitment rather than upon industrial technology. And they would succeed.

Within ten months of commencement of these massive projects, six buildings went up along the sides of the Avenue of Eternal Peace, and two others were constructed in other parts of the city. They created a socialist showpiece that for more than thirty years would cover over and mask a socialist secret of disaster. Once the stories of Great Leap starvation, death, and cannibalism were finally revealed, the sacrifices made in this construction project were all but forgotten in the rush to condemn the overall Maoist political campaign. As a result, this stupendous work became a forgotten footnote to a time that would later be remembered only for the death and destruction it caused. Rather perversely, the same cannot be said of the later Cultural Revolution.

Enveloping China from 1966 to 1976, the Cultural Revolution is remembered chiefly for the destruction caused by rampaging Red Guards. During that decade, what little "showcase" construction occurred was undertaken largely in an environment of secrecy.[22] The political passion that had driven the building boom of the Great Leap appeared to swing back toward revolutionary destruction. By 1966, it was a passion to overthrow the old, not build the new, that spilled out into the streets of Beijing. Red Guards, not building workers, now dominated the now rather inappropriately named Avenue of Eternal Peace.

In the summer and autumn of 1966, word went out among the millions of Red Guards across the country that Mao was personally receiving them in Tiananmen Square. From all across the country, Red Guards descended upon Beijing. All trains, it seemed, led to the Avenue of Eternal Peace. Free trains were provided to transport the Red Guards to meet their Chairman. As they disgorged onto the platforms of the model Beijing Railway Station, the crowds slowly made their way up the Avenue of Eternal Peace toward the open expanse of Tiananmen Square. There, in a sea of red, the Chairman looked down from the balcony of Tiananmen Gate. In a series of reviews, Mao saluted the millions of footsoldiers of his new Cultural Revolution.

Not twenty years earlier, Mao had stood before a previous generation of revolutionaries and announced the establishment of the People's Republic. The gate on which he had stood had been immortalized on the first bank note. It was where Mao's massive picture was hung, and it was also where, in 1966, he was launching his second revolution. As he stood in front of the adoring thousands of Red Guards, he felt the ground move beneath his feet. But the reason was less the adoring crowd than damaged foundations, discovered in the early 1960s. Engineers confirmed Mao's fears.[23] This gateway, which had stood for 550 years and heralded so much of the recent revolutionary history, was now sinking under its own weight.

As a result of the Xintai earthquake of March 1966, the Gate of Heavenly Peace could no longer be left unattended. It was no longer symmetrical, its foundations had sunk, and it was starting to break up. Demolition was the only option, but that option was politically unacceptable. Mythology and politics, as well as time and place, all conspired against any decision to demolish this structure. With the Cultural Revolution having only just been launched from its balcony, the gate was a symbol not only of New China but also of this new movement. To demolish such a structure would have serious symbolic repercussions for any regime. Even the atheistic socialism of Maoism was still hostage to a key element of traditional Chinese statecraft—the notion that legitimacy derived from the will of heaven.

In the traditional cosmology, there was a metonymic link between natural disasters and rule on earth: a natural disaster was symptomatic of a loss of the mandate of heaven. Disasters showed that the gods had turned against the ruler; they were portents of a need for what we call today "regime change." Coming at the very beginning of the Cultural Revolution, this classic sign of impending disaster amounted to a mandate for secrecy. Chinese Communists may well have publicly dismissed traditional cosmological readings of the auspicious and the inauspicious, but they were not prepared to risk the future of the regime. Both the problems afflicting the gate and the solution devised to address them would remain secret for more than thirty years.

The chief problem was both political and logistical: How does one keep a secret in a public square in the center of a bustling capital? To effect the impossible, the regime settled on the bizarre. It would mobilize only its most trusted of model workers; people it knew would work with commitment and passion and would keep a Party secret. As with the Ten Great Projects, the Party would rely upon passion, sacrifice, and political intensity, only this time they would also demand of the workers that they keep the tasks born of commitment a secret. The work plan involved the total demolition of the Gate of Heavenly Peace and its replacement with an exact replica!

So it was that on 15 December 1969 a secret plan came into effect that would see the demolition of the old structure and the construction of a new, nearly identical one. A special work group, affiliated with the military, was commissioned to undertake this task. Eight days later an encasement completely covering the 66 × 37 × 32–meter structure was put in place, and demolition work commenced almost immediately.[24]

In the center of Beijing, under cover of tarpaulins, 2,700 workers dismantled the old gate and constructed an exact replica; and they did it all without breathing a word! As a reward for their diligence and their silence, each worker was given a framed saying about the imperatives of socialism handwritten by the Chairman himself.[25] Each could feel proud of having played a crucial role in Mao's continuous revolution.

That this project was of vital national interest can be gauged by the fact that so many human and material resources were devoted to it. Not only did the project boast an army of the most skilled and dedicated workers; it is said that six kilograms of gold went into making the decorative motifs alone.[26] Time and care were also expended, for example in making sure that the national emblem was exactly aligned with the central point of the traditional south-north axis that ran through the gate. Once a 1.5-ton portrait of Mao was rehung beneath the national emblem, the replica was ready for unveiling to the public, a full two days ahead of schedule.[27]

On 7 March 1970, just 112 days after the project was begun, an exact replica of the gate stood gleaming in the sun. So perfect was this reproduction that most thought that the structure had only been closed for cleaning. The truth would remain a closely guarded secret for the next thirty-three years.[28] Even workers at nearby Zhongshan Park and at the State Construction Ministry knew nothing about this project. Perhaps, in the case of the ministry, their ignorance was understandable. After all, they were probably too busy with a secret construction project of their own to pay much attention to this one.

On 2 March 1969, a Sino-Soviet dispute erupted into violence in the far north of China as Chinese and Soviet troops clashed over rival territorial claims to Zhenbao (Damansky) Island, in the Ussuri River. For the first time, both sides began to imagine the real possibility of a nuclear war. The result was bizarre and erratic behavior. Soviet officials began to "probe" U.S. diplomats to try to find out what the Americans would do if the Soviets launched a preemptive nuclear strike against China's nuclear arsenal;[29] the Chinese prepared against such a strike by initiating what became the major building project of that era. We are, of course, talking about the building of the massive underground city.

Under banners proclaiming the need to "Dig Deep, Prepare Provisions, and Resist Hegemony," an estimated 300,000 Beijing residents would burrow away on this project between 1969 and 1979. The fear of a nuclear winter sent schoolchildren, residents, and army engineers down into these shafts where, it is claimed, they dug tunnels that would stretch for up to thirty kilometers and would be designed to house up to 300,000 people.[30] Lacking both equipment and resources, they used whatever materials were at hand, and the most readily available resource was the old inner-city wall and its towers. In one of those perverse historical twists,

23   Tiananmen Gate as tourist trinket.

the old fortified city wall provided the material for this new underground fortification.

Located approximately eight to ten meters beneath the city's surface, the tunnels are said to contain around 1,000 air-raid shelters, a huge ventilation system with over 2,300 openings, storage facilities that could provide food for residents for two years, and around seventy separate water storage facilities. It has been claimed that the underground city boasted cinemas, classrooms, barbershops, public toilets, a 300-seat theater, and even a 500-bed hospital. These tunnels, covering most of the inner city, were divided into three main parts and had strategic openings within the Forbidden City, the Great Hall, and various government department buildings.[31]

With political considerations driving secrecy in nearly all major construction projects, the prime and most paradoxical exception, the only major public building project undertaken along the Avenue of Eternal Peace in the 1960s and 1970s, was the massive 1973 extension to the old Beijing Hotel.

In the early 1970s more and more visitors were coming to China as the nation began opening up relations with the outside world. This trend was initiated in part by China's growing awareness of its international vulnerability and by its involvement in a cold war with the Soviet Union. By 1971 fifteen countries had switched diplomatic recognition from Taiwan to the People's Republic. The number continued to increase once China took its seat on the United Nations Security Council in October 1971 and began tentatively opening its doors to the outside world.[32]

This was the time of Ping-Pong diplomacy and the beginning of a rapprochement with the United States that would lead to a normalization of diplomatic relations and eventually to the type of investment that would change the face of the city once again. Back in the 1970s, however, it was politics that demanded this opening up, not the need for foreign investment. China needed allies

24   The Beijing Hotel.

against the Soviet Union, and the United States was considered the lesser of two evils. Nevertheless, opening to the outside world had its costs. It created a need for more accommodation to house important foreign dignitaries who were now starting to come to China. As China wanted to present its best face to the outside world, the Beijing Hotel was regarded as the ideal location for foreign guests. Located on the busy shopping street Wangfujing, but facing the Avenue of Eternal Peace, the hotel is only a five-minute walk from Tiananmen Square. Its central location near Tiananmen was ideal, both as a hotel site for important foreign guests and as a political statement. The political statement it would make was that China had finally thrown off the shackles of the colonial era because of the Communist liberation of the city and the country.

The hotel extension could deliver such a message because it would modify the original Beijing Hotel, which had been built by the French in 1900 to house their diplomats and to assert their colonial dominance in the center of the capital. Architecturally, the original structure successfully did both. At that time, its Western style and its height made it stand out, while its sumptuous appointments within made it a perfect and central residence for diplomats. The new wing would accomplish both a pragmatic and a political objective: it would house the increasing number of visiting foreign dignitaries, and it would do so in a way that magnified the dignity of New China by dwarfing the old French structure with a grandeur all its own. It was, in other words, an attempt to create a sort of socialist grandeur.

Zhang Bo, the architect of the Great Hall, was drafted to design the extension, and many features of the Great Hall reappear in the standard modernist hotel building and its elaborate lobby. The extension was originally designed to stand 100 meters high, but fears that it would overlook the Zhongnanhai leadership compound led to a modification that reduced it to approximately

25   The original Beijing Hotel, built by the French in 1900.

80 meters.[33] Even so, it would still dominate the far older and smaller French-built structure, which now became the hotel's west wing.

In many ways the result is a perfect metaphor of late Maoism. It captures an impending change that was about to transform the city once again. Just as the faltering Maoist ring-road construction work was a sign of failed modernity that economic reform would not only finish but also extend, so too the openness of the hotel was something that economic reform would push to the limit. Yet the Beijing Hotel extension was also caught on the cusp of two worlds, two eras, one of them defined by political intrigues and secrets, the other by free-market openness and utility. Built with an overt political purpose, it was conceived along familiar monumental political lines, down to the choice of the architect. Nevertheless, as a hotel wing it was designed specifically to cater to guests, and foreign ones at that. It therefore constitutes a perfect temporal fulcrum between socialist past and free-market future.

The hotel lobby may feature many adornments drawn from the Great Hall, but it is still a hotel lobby. The hotel lobby, in many ways, forms a perfect contrast to the People's Square five minutes away to its west. Like Tiananmen Square, the hotel lobby is specially designed to hold vast numbers of people. Unlike the square, the lobby holds no agenda. The lobby is invariably agnostic about the political beliefs of the crowd. And the only sight aloft that might inspire wonder is a new, exciting, and flagrantly materialist city skyline.

Tiananmen Square is a political space designed to inspire and direct the crowd; the Beijing Hotel, like all the others in the city today, is a space of pure utility. The early boom in hotel construction changed the face of this city and flagged a new way of dealing with the crowd. Within ten years of the construction of the new wing of the Beijing Hotel, a bolder and quite new political flag was being raised over the Avenue of Eternal Peace. If there was a harbinger of economic reform, it came in 1982, with the building of the first jointly owned Sino-U.S. venture, the Jianguo Hotel. Constructed on the symbolically significant extension of the Avenue of Eternal Peace, this hotel marked the new dominance of economic development and opened a path out of the overt political constructions of the Mao era.

Within a year of the Jianguo's completion, the first fully owned foreign venture, the Great Wall Sheraton, went up in nearby Sanlitun, built to coincide with the visit of Ronald Reagan in 1984. Politics, then, still glimmered faintly in the construction of these early hotels. Nevertheless, this was no longer the same politics that had once impelled volunteers to building sites in the time of the Ten Great Projects. Construction, once demanded as an act of political loyalty, had now become a matter of economic necessity. The timely completion of buildings was no longer tied to political events but to contractual obligations. Workers were no longer inspired to work hard from a sense of political commitment; now they were working hard because their wages and bonuses depended upon it. As the boom in hotels continued, the contract, the market, and the economy grew alongside it. As the economy grew in importance, commitment politics withered. In making their mark on the city skyline, these ever-taller, ever more grandiose Western-style hotels also marked out the path traveled from a world dominated by politics to one run by commerce. As this trend intensified, the hotel began to reveal something else.

"The hotel lobby," writes Siegfried Kracauer, is the "inverted image of the house of God."[34] He could just as well have said that it is the inverted image of Tiananmen Square in 1966 or of the construction sites of the Ten Great Projects in 1958. There is still something nonmaterialist, almost mystical, in the political inspiration behind the Maoist projects. The flow of spirit, though reoriented along a different axis, still flowed in the Mao era.

The spirit of Maoism forged a society around a sense of struggle by promising a world beyond measure. Like religion, commitment politics raised questions about purposefulness, about the absolute, and also about limit. The Communist Party transformed everyday issues into a symbolic language of class. "The people-as-one before their supreme Other" is how Claude Lefort once described this inspirational form.[35] He could have been speaking about the Red Guards in Tiananmen Square or about Kracauer's church congregation. After all, as Kracauer notes, "only those who stand before God are sufficiently estranged from one another to discover they are brothers."[36] As this brotherhood was transformed into comradeship, it produced a way of being a new socialist person. It could attract and repel, give life yet cause death, and bring forth the worst of results with the very best of intentions. In other words, it was a form of "collectivity" that was the antithesis of the cold, businesslike "individualism" that one finds manifest in the hotel lobby.

In the hotel lobby, "Instead of guiding people beyond themselves, the mystery slips between the masks," says Kracauer.[37] The hotel lobby is a place not of enchantment but of tuxedos, a world not where one is burned by a brighter, higher light, but where one is instead drawn into a land of registration counters and orderly queues, or, in the words of Kracauer, "the inessential foundation at the basis of rational socialization."[38] The lobby offers anonymity in the crowd rather than leading the crowd toward a sense of collectivity in which each person becomes part of a collective dream of "the we." There can be no spirit of "we-ness" in the hotel crowd, for everyone is there on business. Yet what of those who come for pleasure, to see, for example, the Olympics? Here, in the crowd that comes for a sporting event, we might still find, as Norbert Elias and Eric Dunning did, a faint glimmer of the spirit of the political collective. Yet it is a very different sort of collectivity being experienced and enacted here. In place of Red Guards massed before their great leader, first chanting, then violently enacting the revolutionary line, we see the stadium crowd roaring in support of their team. With their passions expended on sport, there is less intensity left for politics. Politics no longer galvanizes people to committed, purposeful action; it now dulls them through regulation and legislation.

Elias and Dunning saw the virtues of this dulling effect. Indeed, Elias came to regard it as part of what he famously called the "civilizing process." Organized sport, Elias and Dunning claimed, had a calming effect on the crowd and played an often-underrecognized role in overcoming the "cycles of violence" that politics produces—the either/or politics that found expression in the Tiananmen Square of the Red Guards. In place of commitment politics we find the rise of what Elias and Dunning called "parliamentarization."[39] It is as though the rules of the game now apply to both sports and politics.

Both parliamentary politics and team sport might still crave an either/or result, and the fight to achieve it may well raise the passions, but, even as it rises to a crescendo in the sports stadium, it still observes an absolute obedience to the rules of the game. Slowly, the limitless intensity of the "we" of the political rally is turning into the roar of dedicated fans as the rules of the game are imposed upon them. Once these various areas of life are rule-bound, their area of jurisdiction dictates their application. Sport becomes a discrete domain, cut off from everyday life and converted into a special event. It always knows limit, for it lives by the time limits of the starter's gun and the final whistle. Yet there are ways in which this "we" of the sporting crowd constantly outflanks the maneuvers and mechanisms designed to corral it. This, at least, is what major sporting events teach us.

Although any sporting event can be understood in terms of Elias and Dunning's analysis, there is more to the Olympics than their analysis would admit. The Olympics are never just about sport. For the host city, the Olympics are less about the pacifying effects of the stadium crowd than about the rousing effects of national pride. Olympic stadiums characteristically become high-technology symbols of nationhood. In Beijing, these bold sporting-design statements are put on display alongside the new National Grand Theater and the CCTV Center to present a paradox: postmodern design is pressed into the service of that very modernist notion, nationalism. It is nationalism built on a confidence that comes with the acquisition of awesome economic power. Together they have become symbols of the new postreform China just as the Ten Great Projects were symbols of the era of the Maoist socialist state.

Yet what was interesting about the building of the Ten Great Projects, we discovered, was not their look but their builders' outlook. What, then, is the outlook of the contemporary builder of, say, the CCTV Center? The construction workers of the new Beijing have come, like the 1950s workers before them, in the hundreds of thousands to build this New Jerusalem. The difference lies in the fact that this latest version of Jerusalem is being built not from a sense of political commitment but on the basis of an economic contract.

"How long are you here for?" we yell across to a Hunanese worker on the CCTV construction site. "One year . . . one-year contracts," he yells back, trying to be heard above the din of the work. "We are all here on one-year contracts!" he adds. He swings away from us and back to work. He has to, for in this new way of work in contemporary China, time is money. Ten months left to complete the work; otherwise they will be in breach of contract. Back to work they go. They are too busy to think of anything else. There is no political dream left on these building sites, just as there is no "we-ness" in the crowd in the hotel lobby. Yet there is still something left over from that dream, a vestige of that spirit of kinship, but one now unconnected to the roar of the crowd.

So let us try to find this spirit, not in the roar of the crowd or in the violence of the Red Guards, but in a quieter form of "we-ness" produced in affective communities. Let us venture to a place where a sense of the collective still softly touches the shoulders of the people, where the starkness of the choice between Tiananmen and the hotel lobby breaks down into fragments, where comradeliness still mixes with cash registers, markets, and everyday life. This is a place for which no monuments will be built or streetscapes re-rendered. It may not shine bright against the city's night sky as economic reform does, but there is something of a gentle glow flowing from a sense of community. The older suburb of Jiaodaokou still has within it that sense of place, of community. We can see this suburb of gray-tiled old-fashioned rundown buildings from the Urban Exhibition Center, but that perspective will not capture a sense of community or collective. For that, we must venture onto the street.

"The power of a country road," writes Walter Benjamin, "is different when one is walking along it from when one is flying over it by airplane . . . The airplane passenger sees only how the road pushes through the landscape, how it unfolds according to the same laws as the terrain surrounding it. Only he who walks the road on foot learns of the power it commands, and of how, from the very scenery that for the flier is only the unfurled plain, it calls forth distances, belvedere, clearings, prospects at each of its turns like a commander deploying soldiers to the front."[40] For Benjamin, this was a metaphor to explain the differences between reading a book and copying it. Copying marks the mind, while reading, he suggested, gives an overview.

Let us take a leaf out of Benjamin's book and follow the style of the copyist, but let us take this style not back into the text, but for a walk down the street. Let us speak to the people as we pass their homes and move from the grandiose symbols of national and political power to the simpler expressions of the state at its lower branches. Let these voices guide us toward that faint whisper of a politics of we-ness. It's a politics no longer expressed as politics, for it has been habituated into a way of life. Let us trace this collective sense of we-ness, not into grand political statements of "we Chinese," but down small alleyways where we find neighborhood committees, community actions, and a more localized sense of being. Let us, with these thoughts, venture into the backstreets of Jiaodaokou.

3 THE COMMUNITY

"It was different back then," says Liu Zhengxian as he takes another drag on his Panda cigarette and gazes into the air, reflecting upon a time now dismissed by Chinese and Westerners alike as simply "ten years of chaos."[1] Flanked on one side by a large picture of the Great Wall and on the other by the hammer-and-sickle-embossed red flag of the Communist Party, Liu sits in the meeting room of a police station he once ran and retells stories of his life as the deputy police chief in a suburb called Jiaodaokou.

Located just northwest of Tiananmen Square and adjacent to the now-glamorous tourist-bar and nightclub area of Houhai, Jiaodaokou is home to over 50,000 people who live in approximately 20,000 often-cramped low-rise compound households covering approximately 1.47 square kilometers of the inner-city police precinct. The suburb is split into ten areas or communities (shequs) consisting largely of around half a dozen hutongs, or alleyways, each housing some 5,000 people.

From the time of the Cultural Revolution right up until the 1990s, Liu was in charge of them all. This was his small patch of the revolution.

Over the years Jiaodaokou became not just his personal contribution to the revolutionary cause, but his home. Little wonder, then, that when he finally stopped wearing the uniform of authority, Jiaodaokou became his retirement village. Many of the residents now living in the cramped compound households of Jiaodaokou are also retired. Indeed, these days, it is only when these older residents "move upstairs," as the colloquial expression for moving into high-rise apartments has it, that different, largely younger people get a chance to move in.

While a wealthy few have moved in and restored some of the old compound houses to their former dynastic glory, most of these remain as they were immediately after the revolution. That is, they are cramped, dilapidated spaces organized to house many in a space originally designed and built for the use of an elite few. It is

26   Liu Zhengxian.

into these old, patched-up, rundown compound houses that poor migrants, eager for work in the "big smoke," have moved.

Whether they are rich young city go-getters or down-at-heel rustics on the make, it's likely that the young people we see in this part of town aren't originally from around here. The result is a suburb in which outsiders and insiders, young and old, as well as rich and poor, live cheek by jowl. In this respect at least, there is continuity with the past, for Jiaodaokou has always been a suburb of extremes. It was certainly that way before the revolution.

"Before the revolution," Liu tells us, "this used to be the suburb of brothels and coffinmakers." He points across the police station courtyard in the direction of Chaodou Alleyway. "There used to be a brothel over there," he says somewhat whimsically. Then, turning in the other direction, toward two of the suburb's main streets, he stabs a finger into the air saying, "And over there, in Jiaodaokou Dongdajie, and also over there, in Nanluo Guxiangwai, there used to be row upon row of coffinmakers." Clearly, sex and death were on close terms in Jiaodaokou. The presence of coffinmakers is hardly surprising given the history of the place. In imperial times, Jiaodaokou had, after all, been an execution ground.

In most respects Jiaodaokou's past, like the criminals executed there, has long since been buried and forgotten. These days, only one version of the past survives in this suburb, consisting of two landmarks of national significance on its northern perimeter. These two landmarks—the Bell Tower and the Drum Tower—not only mark the northernmost limits of Jiaodaokou but, as we have already seen, also delimited daily dynastic time.

Jiaodaokou may no longer awaken to the chimes from the ancient bells or move through the day to the beat of an ancient drum, but we can still imagine the flow of spirit, or *qi*, through its now half-derelict alleyways and into the old *siheyuans,* or compound households. A walk down any one of these old narrow *hutongs* will yield a glimpse of this past as it lives on in faded glory.

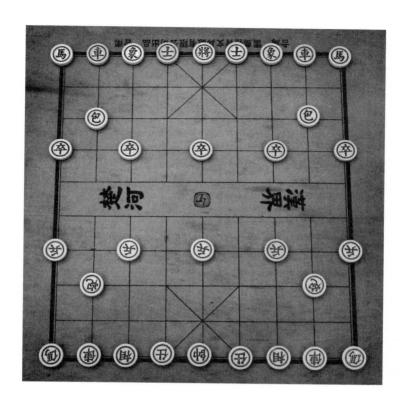

27   A Chinese chessboard.

Ignore the shabby street signs in broken English, the piles of rubbish and knots of traffic that are so much part of the new consumer world, and forget, momentarily, the walls that have been punctured to make a space for large shop windows. Imagine, instead, a Jiaodaokou of yesteryear, as a single square on a Chinese chessboard of life that is as old as the city itself.

"The layout of the city is like a chessboard, with every *siheyuan* being a piece on that board," writes Gao Wei. "Every piece has a particular, ordered place, which reflected the strict, regulated life of propriety that was the basis of the Confucian order."[2] Chess isn't a bad image to begin with to think about this city, its houses, and its past life. It is an even better metaphor when we begin to reflect upon specific parts of the built environment, such as the beams and gables at the entranceways into compound households, and of the logic that lies behind the use of those gables and beams.

At the outermost corners of any chessboard's back row sit the castles, then, in an inward progression, the knights, and, closest to the king, the bishops. In Chinese chess, there is no queen, only the Praetorian Guard, whose sole purpose is to protect the inner sanctum of empire where imperial power and the emperor reside. We can perhaps imagine this as the Forbidden City of Chinese chess. Nine pieces are ordered along the back row of the Chinese chessboard. Nine beams protrude from above the entranceways into the Forbidden City. This likeness is not fortuitous.

Such beams and gables, called *menzans* or *mendings*, featured atop every doorway entrance to every courtyard household entrance of officials in the whole of imperial China. Jiaodaokou had few families of great rank, so in the small compound households of this suburb we find mostly only two beams and very occasionally four protruding from the gateway entrances. On each beam, like the characters carved onto the surface of a Chinese chesspiece, we often find calligraphy. Now dusty and worn, these engravings still reveal the characters for longevity (*fushou*), auspiciousness *(jixiang)*, and harmony *(ping'an)*. For those with higher status and more beams, more characters would have been etched onto the surface, in the hope that these would bring even more good fortune: "One gate with five blessings" *(wufu)*—longevity, fortune, harmony, security, and a blessed death—featured on some, while other households merely desired "safety in and out" *(churu ping'an)*.

Beneath the beams above the entrance, the gates themselves are often ornate. Invariably painted red for happiness, the gates always opened in the middle—a deliberate arrangement to reflect the two-sided quality of the notion of harmony, which must always involve a balance of forces. Whether on beams, gates, or the written banners called *duilian* hung on both sides of the gateway or doorway, the balancing of *yin* and *yang* must always prevail. All things were arranged in a way to bring forth harmony. The *duilian*, poetic couplets written in the ancient ornate Chinese script, described the status, nature, or role of the occupants within. "Gathering all blessings; graciously endowed with good omens" would flag the home of a low-ranking official, while "Splendid civilization of the ancient empire; new civilians of great advancement" would announce the presence of a court official. Powerful merchants also marked their doors with calligraphy, in the belief that prosperity flowed from couplets such as "Reinvigorating family enterprise and generating handsome wealth."

If merchants desired prosperity and the nobility health, all households, whatever their rank or status, desired fertility. The importance of the concept of a family line in China demanded nothing less. Although many people of Chinese descent living in Western countries now put their family names last, in China the traditional practice of writing the family name first attests to the persisting importance of an unbroken family line. In this tradition, the desire for continuity was so strong that symbols of fertility were ubiquitous. One example survives on the gateway entrance,

28   Left: a traditional compound doorway.

Right: the locked entrance to a security courtyard (*an'quan yuan*).

29   Doorknobs celebrating fertility.

30   A stone pier *(mendun)*.

where circular protruding doorknobs jut out in the same way that a young woman's breasts might protrude from her body. Some knobs displayed patterns referred to as "girdles" *(dudous)*. Patterned or not, the knobs carried the auspicious meaning *shidai zhuancheng*, "the family line will continue from one generation to the next."

At the foot of any gateway is a pair of small stone piers *(menduns)* rendered into the shape of either a rectangular pedestal *(menzuo, mentai, menzhen)* or a round drum *(baoshigu or mengu)*. These, too, flagged the power and status of the residents. A circular surface carving represented a drum, which symbolized the beat of war and marked out the households of noble warriors of rank, or *wu*. A rectangular shape represented an inkpad and thus indicated the presence of a noble family of letters, or *wen*. The sides of these stone carvings were often covered with auspicious decoration. Some featured the *bagua* of the *I Ching (Yiqing)*, others featured a lion king, and still others might be decorated with a design based on bamboo shoots. In all cases, however, strength, temperance, and stability were the meanings being conveyed.

Every courtyard door has a thick wooden timber across the threshold. Evil spirits, it seemed, could not overstep this mark. Just in case they did, behind each gate, and separating the entrance from the courtyard within, there was often a "spirit wall" *(yingbi)* that further hindered or blocked the progress of bad *qi*.

The walls and tiles of most compound houses in Jiaodaokou are gray. This was the color of the ordinary people. Very occasionally, the gray is punctuated by the glimmer of green glazed tiles on the roofs of formerly noble households. In this suburb, however, we will never find the glorious golden glazed tiles reserved for the home of the emperor. To gaze at that color we must move across this chessboard of a city to the Imperial Palace with its nine beamed entranceways.

31   Tricycle tours of old Beijing.

The persistence and power of the ancient cosmology in Jiao-daokou have moved the Chinese tourist authorities to designate it a "conservation zone." Laborers now toil here night and day, restoring the old alleyways to their former glory and also adding impressive new "traditional style" public toilet blocks complete with running water. To accommodate the influx of tourists, tricycle businesses have set up shop here offering "*hutong* tours of old Beijing."

Tourists are now venturing in ever-greater numbers into areas like the restored Yuan'en Temple area of western Jiaodaokou, which is where most of the (re)construction work is taking place. Yet on their way into this slice of "old Beijing," the tricycles now pass discreet but very trendy cocktail bars, expensive fashion houses, and restaurants, as well as slick cafés advertising free wireless services with their coffee. Clearly, these Wi-Fi cafés and other businesses have picked up the signals that tourist dollars are beaming their way.

There is, then, a paradox built into the survival of this traditional suburb. It is a tradition being rebuilt for a very modern purpose, tourism. Indeed, tourism is in danger of turning parts of this place into a Chinese version of Disneyland. Yet although we do indeed catch a glimpse of old Beijing here, just beneath the surface of this tourist-friendly place there is a different version of old Beijing being played out. This is not the "old Beijing" that the tourist board wants to sell, but one it wants to occlude.

This is the old Beijing of the Maoist era. The community campaign now being mounted to "traditionalize" this suburb is being carried out with all the enthusiasm of the Maoist political campaigns of old. In addition to tourist-board money, the mass-line neighborhood committee has also been mobilized. This time, however, cleaning up the streets, not cleaning out "bad elements," is their goal. We are able to meet with them through the good offices of the Yuan'en Temple area committee head, Sister Xu, who invites

32   Inside the trendy Guogeba (Passerby Bar), Jiaodaokou.

us to one of her meetings and, en route, tells us about her greatest achievements and greatest challenges.

Our guide tells us of her strong desire to have Jiaodaokou crowned a "national civilized city area," a distinction that, she hints, is the suburban equivalent of winning an Academy Award. In many ways she is closer to the filmic mark than she thinks, for this area is trying very hard to act the part of an ancient suburb. Indeed, like Shu Qi in Hou Xiaoxian's film, *Three Times* (2005), this suburb operates across three different temporal zones.

In *Three Times*, Shu Qi plays the part of a woman in dynastic China, then in the 1960s, and finally in the contemporary era. In the Yuan'en Temple area, the streets play their part in mimicking dynastic Beijing, while renovations are carried out through the efforts of Maoist mass-line activists. All this is being done in order to get resources into the area and boost its capitalist land value. There is a lot riding on gaining the award, and Sister Xu is quick to tell us that her closest rivals come from Beijing's western suburbs. She is confident, though, that she will win, for, like all good strategists, she has at her disposal a secret weapon.

"We are a bit behind in the provision of facilities at the moment," she admits, "but I'm not worried, because we have something the Western suburbs don't have. We have the best people!" As the head of the key mass-line organization of this area, it is good that she displays such faith in the local masses; she is going to need it. "The authorities went to Ju'er Lane for the first round of this competition," she tells us. "But you know, visiting there might just have been a cover, because everyone knows that this competition will be won or lost not by open competition but by *mincha anfang* [official investigation and secret checking].

"On the afternoon of 30 April the inspections began, but we were onto their ruse from the very start," she proudly states. "Residents came running to my office to tell me that the people's consultative committee chairman and his people were not just in

Ju'er Lane but were carrying out checks elsewhere. It turns out that they conducted secret investigations in three of our other alleyways: Houyuansi, Qianyuansi, and Qinglao *hutongs*. They secretly had a look around these three places, and their verdict . . . well . . . it was excellent really. In fact, we had a total victory! After that our spirits rose because we knew we were in with a real shot at the big prize.

"Then, on 9 May, another team arrived to secretly check up on us. This time, however, they were interested less in the built environment than they were in community spirit. They went around asking locals whether or not they knew that our area was up for the award of best city area in the nation. Of course, everybody knew. Such a big deal, how could they not? But what was really pleasing was the impression they left on the investigating team. Apparently my residents started to thank the team members profusely for their interest. They began saying things like 'We offer our heartfelt gratitude to you,' and so forth. Now when I heard that, I was really touched. In fact, I still get goose bumps every time I think about it! After that, I knew that I wasn't wasting my time with this area, this work, and this competition. As a result of that last check, we were named a focal area, and people started getting excited but also getting very nervous. It's funny, you know, the closer you get to victory, the more anxious some people become; but, for my part, I was just happy that we had got this far.

"Look at this," she says, pointing to her arm. "I'm covered in goose bumps again just thinking about this." She invites us to accompany her to a meeting of about twenty "activists." Most of these activists turn out to be septuagenarians long since retired from Party service but now forming the backbone of the Yuan'en Temple neighborhood committee. The meeting was convened primarily to discuss strategy for the next round of competition.

Things are a little tense as we join the meeting along with the young and handsome community police officer in charge of this

33   Policeman Bai talks to the Yuan'en Temple area neighborhood committee

in a breezy Chinese courtyard on a hot summer's day.

area, Xiao Bai. New to the area and to policing generally, Xiao Bai has come to discuss the security aspect of the competition. "After all, to win best area, you have to have low crime," Xiao Bai tells us before he addresses the small and aged crowd. So here we are, sitting under leafy vines strung across a latticework-covered courtyard, while Xiao Bai explains to this pensioner army of activists what they can do to achieve their campaign goal.

"Hi, everybody," says Xiao Bai. "Despite the fact that I'm relatively new here, I guess there's no need for me to introduce myself, is there?" he asks rhetorically, with a knowing smile. There is no response, just silence and anticipation. "So let me get straight into it, then, shall we?" Silence again follows. "I've just come to remind you all that I am here to help, and what I need in return is your help. So please support me by making sure that all windows stay closed and locked in the following months to ensure there are no thefts during the time of competition." There is a muffled chortle among the ranks. "It's clear that he doesn't live in a compound house," one woman comments, while another points out to her friend that these traditional courtyard compounds are specifically designed to let the breeze flow through in summer to offer relief from the stifling heat. One wit gets everybody going: "I know we all said we would win the competition or die trying, but I never imagined you'd take this literally and suggest we all die of heatstroke!" he yells. As the nods of dissent burble over into laughter, our hostess steps in to silence the crowd.

In another era she would have been called a "Marxism-Leninism old lady," but these days such terms no longer apply. She may be as pushy and domineering as the M-L ladies of old, but these days it's civilized behavior, not class struggle, that she's pushing. Right now, she's pushing to save the beleaguered Xiao Bai.

"Hey, come on, everybody, how about giving a bit of support to Xiao Bai?" she says. "Okay, he lives in an apartment, not a compound house, but, even so, he lives miles from here and yet still makes an effort to be available twenty-four/seven. He is really hard-working, so how about showing him a little bit more support? Okay, I know that in summertime everybody likes to open their doors and windows and sleep outside because of the heat, but if you won't lock things up, then how are we going to get through the competition security checks? Okay, if locking up is no good, how about getting people to consider putting bars on their windows? If anyone has a problem with that, just ask him or her to come and see me. And if someone can't manage to put bars on their windows, then that's fine, too, because we can always bring in a worker to do that for them." She changes tone as she moves from castigating the crowd about their treatment of Xiao Bai to cajoling them into action.

"The thing is," she begins, "we can't afford to lose this competition over this issue. Remember the competition is really heating up. There are 137 communities competing for this award, and now that we've been designated a focal area, we have a really good shot at winning this competition. So let's not blow it all by slacking off now." She perfunctorily repeats Xiao Bai's line about security, but that is just a segue to where she really wants to be. "So, yes, let's listen to Xiao Bai. After all, he's a policeman, and policemen know about these things. Let's make sure that doors are kept shut when they're supposed to be shut, but, most important of all, let's also make sure that when compound households in our area are in need of repair, they get fixed up. If you notice any of the walls in any of our hutongs that are in need of a coat of paint, then get to it and paint them.

"We're doing okay, you know. I can now officially report to you that the new public toilet blocks have proven a great success. Beijing's hygiene checks have been carried out in our area recently and it showed that we are in really good shape on that front."[3]

There is a murmur of satisfaction, and a new air of confidence and determination begins to run through this aged crowd. Suddenly the mood has lifted, and everyone seems to be getting back on track.

"As for security, well, we are doing well there, too. Most of our residents are still living in compound households, and their attitude to crime prevention has been really good. In fact, the crime rate in our area is still the lowest." Xiao Bai nods in agreement, and a collective smile passes like a Mexican wave through the crowd.

Our guide continues with even more gusto: "The attitude of the majority of our residents really pleases me and fills me with pride. So, as the head of this great area, I must bow before you all and say thank you; thank you, everyone. Thank you for your efforts, for your vigilance, and for your support. Please keep reminding people about the competition. That's crucial. Make sure that all residents know that when the inspectors come around they need to be ready and primed to perform. Remember, one key criterion of this competition is that residents must be civilized and polite. So it's up to you to communicate this to your families, to your neighborhood, and to your friends. Politeness really doesn't take much effort. In fact, it simply means sticking to our old traditions. For example, I find it particularly heartwarming when I'm greeted with the old courtesies, like 'Have you eaten yet?' and so forth. We need to maintain or retrieve this kind of polite, warm language, and if it comes down to a choice between the formal and the familiar, I'd always choose the former, just to be on the safe side. By doing this, we can harmonize the relationships among humans and between humans and nature. That way, our community, too, can become harmonious."

Then, to show that she is doing her bit on that front, she quickly adds: "For the sake of harmony, I've organized a 'harmonious community sing-along' right here in this courtyard on 27

May. I want you all to come along and to get everyone else to come along too. We shall all sing together. I think that through collective song, we will manage to reach the harmonious aims we have set for ourselves. Our area, our leaders, our work units, and our families are all very different, but when we all happily sing and relax together, we learn the importance of singing from the same hymnsheet. And that, comrades, is how we are going to win this competition! Thank you!"

The small crowd applauds. With this rousing speech, the struggle for harmony in the Yuan'en Temple area is assured for another day. But although their leader delights in the progress being made, she is also painfully aware of the little things that could still trip up her vision of success. As she hands the floor over to her security chief, it is tripping of a different kind that takes center stage.

Addressing the mostly elderly ladies before her, the security chief warns that when they are on patrol they should refrain from wearing slippers. "If faced with an emergency, how can you run in slippers?" she asks rhetorically. In this group, the wearing of slippers doesn't seem to be the main impediment to running.

The neighborhood committee security chief continues with a long list of "nos." On childcare: "Don't take your grandchildren out on patrol with you. You are a mass-line organization, not a childcare service. Again, if there's an emergency, how can you adequately respond if you are holding a baby or holding the hand of a toddler?" she asks. The security chief saves her most important point until last: "Most of all, don't forget to wear your red armbands! While on duty they must be worn," she says. Those without armbands start to shuffle uncomfortably, and a pointing of fingers and wagging of tongues come from those who have remembered theirs. Like the area leader, the security chief tries to end on a strong note, but her crescendo strikes slightly false:

34   One of the ubiquitous red armbands of the neighborhood security committee.

"You can't say these armbands are bad, because these little bands are unique to China! In fact, even their red color is unique to China. If a bad person sees one of these little bands, they'll get very nervous! These armbands boost your power and are a symbol of pride, so wear them with pride!" she shouts as she works herself up as though this is a matter of great political urgency. A trickle of applause follows before the meeting breaks up and the patrols set off to inspect the *hutongs* and gateways of the area.

Off goes this ragtag army of septuagenarians, shuffling along in slippers, with the occasional flash of a red armband. Here we are with them, joining the last, aging remnants of that other "old Beijing." This is an old Beijing that no one really wants to remember these days and certainly no tourist ever wants to visit. Yet this old Beijing still colonizes a popular mind-set even in the flashy Yuan'en Temple area. It is an old Beijing that leads us all the way back to the stories of Liu Zhengxian. It leads us back into a Jiaodaokou he once patrolled where much more than the gateway entrances into the compound houses was being painted red.

"Everything was red back then," Liu states as he mutters "ultra-left" (*jizuo fenzi*) under his breath before breaking into yet another story of Jiaodaokou during the Cultural Revolution. "You know, these days, no one really remembers what happened back then," he says as he starts to fill us in on what the tourist brochures for the area don't reveal.

In what was a very different but no less radical "renovation" of Jiaodaokou, he tells us how everything turned red at this time, including the street names. "In Jiaodaokou, they didn't change the street names back to the old names until 1980. It was at that time that a special committee of the city council was put in charge of the rectification of names. Only then did they go back to using the old names," he explains. "Back in the Cultural Revolution, though, many of these older *hutongs* were given new revolutionary names," he adds with a smile.

The renaming of streets during the Cultural Revolution was, of course, not confined to Jiaodaokou but took place throughout the city. Perhaps the most provocative and famous of these renamings was one that concerned the street on which the then-Soviet (now Russian) embassy was located. Its address from 1968 into 1969 was Number One, Antirevisionist Lane, Beijing! Who says Maoism didn't have a sense of humor! Jiaodaokou, like every other suburb in the city, underwent a similar rectification. Dou Family Alleyway became Red-All-the-Way Lane, while Earth Child Alleyway was renamed Overcome Lane. "Even the name of the main street of Jiaodaokou was changed," Liu adds. "What is now Jiaonankou High Street was turned into Great Leap Forward Road." Today these changes are, politically, all but unspeakable, and they exist only in the memories of people like Liu.

Gesturing now across the room, out the window, to the street in front of the station, Liu says with a smile that breaks into a chortle: "D'you know what that one, out there, was called during the Cultural Revolution? Well, that was called Study Mao Lane!" His huge grin looks like the smile of a guilty child as he again mutters under his breath "ultra-left." He then turns to the others in the room, who smile along with him; suddenly, like a bursting dam, all break into peals of laughter. It is embarrassed laughter, confused laughter; it's cover-up laughter, laughter designed to paper over the fact that in these days of rampant market development, the rectification of names in the Cultural Revolution seems almost too absurd to be believed. They laugh because they know that not so very long ago, this really was no laughing matter. Yet their laughter throws up a paradox about this faintly absurdist theater that is being performed in Jiaodaokou. Here we sit, in a suburb trying so very hard to resurrect its distant past but simultaneously trying just as hard to bury and erase its more recent one.

As we look out on the bustling thoroughfare that once went by the name Study Mao Lane and see the hawkers selling their wares,

35   The poster says: "Completely clean out the reactionary clique of Hu

Feng and all other secret counterrevolutionaries."

the restaurant billboards advertising expensive local cuisines, and the occasional backpacker venturing up to the youth hostel near the corner, we realize that in this part of "old Beijing" there is quite a bit of the past that is being cut from history's pages to make way for a newer version of the old.

"Nobody knows about these things anymore, and if you want to look them up, you can't, because there are no records," Liu sighs, suddenly turning serious after his moment of frivolity. He shakes his head as though the lack of records has robbed him personally of his own time and history. In many ways, it has. This is because it isn't just the rectification of street names that has been erased from history's pages; all manner of things that flowed from the Cultural Revolution period are now repressed. Not only is the Cultural Revolution the great politically unspeakable moment, but also there are no records of this period that would help that unspeakable moment ever regain its voice. Barely spoken of and largely unrecorded, that era is now being airbrushed from history's pages. Perhaps no one knows the consequences of this airbrush technique on history better than Liu. This is because, immediately before his time in Jiaodaokou, Liu had been one of the key Party experts on the use of the airbrush upon historical actors.

He gained this expertise at a time when most of his police comrades in the Ministry of Public Security and in the Beijing Police Bureau were being purged and banished. That was when Liu was called into police headquarters and given a secret mission: Go through the records of senior political and police figures held in the archives of the Police Bureau and the ministry and find evidence of counterrevolutionary crimes that would justify the erasure of these people from history's recordbook.

Liu was given the file of Hu Feng, a major literary and cultural figure first purged in 1955 and up for renewed attack in the throes of the Cultural Revolution, to work on. "Completely clean out the reactionary clique of Hu Feng and all other secret counterrevolutionaries" were Liu's instructions. He was put in a room full of documents on Hu and told to get started. "I had a whole room full of files and records just on him and his clique to go through," Liu tells us. "Imagine that; all these documents, just on him! There were piles and piles of stuff, and every one of them, I've read," he says in a rather matter-of-fact way.

Liu's Cultural Revolution job was as ancient as the alleyways of Jiaodaokou. In being brought into police headquarters and given access to records, registers, and files to help the powerful to defeat their rivals, Liu was performing a time-honored traditional function. In China the use of records has always played a pivotal role in the accession of new regimes to power. It is said that when Han armies sacked the Qin capital and formed the new Han state in 206 B.C., the first thing the new chief of staff did was not to loot the national treasures, but to secure its records.[4] Little had changed two millennia later, even though the Cultural Revolution was openly declaring warfare upon all things traditional.

Liu would do this job for almost two years. He was there to help, he said, to do his duty, to serve the people; but we sense that there was something more than duty and service at play here. Possibly there was a certain intoxication flowing from being this close to power, and some sense of his own power derived from playing a key role in bringing down the powerful. But being that close to power in China would also be a source of great anxiety and even fear.

To know that the powerful could fall so hard, so quickly, and so easily must have acted as a chilling reminder to Liu of his own utter expendability. "You have to understand; we were under enormous pressure," says Liu. "Chairman Mao visited all the research groups cleaning out the Party. We all met him at the Workers' Stadium. And people like Madame Mao and others from the Cultural Revolution group pressured us all the time to get more denunciation material faster."

Under such pressure, Liu and the other researchers from the four groups cleaning out the Party would airbrush and scalpel their way through famous people's lives until they had rendered the meritorious as being without merit. The damning indictments would then be passed on to the higher authorities, who would in turn leak them to the Red Guard groups, who would publicly broadcast them and use them to drag people out. Later, Chinese would use an old expression to describe this process: *duanzhan quyi,* or "taking things out of context." Liu uses this expression over and over again in our conversation with him. The consequences were dire for those named. In Beijing's public security arena alone, 5,700 people were convicted of counterrevolutionary crimes largely on the basis of evidence drawn from their personnel files.

For almost two years these files were worked on and their victims airbrushed into nonexistence until finally, in 1969, Party purging gave way to Party reconsolidation, and the cadres whose lives had been almost ruined by smear and innuendo made it out of the cowshed and back into power. They would have their revenge upon the files that had damned them. It was now the turn of their files— the very things that had been used to denounce them—to be sent down to the countryside.

So it was that in 1969 the airbrush and scalpel were replaced by the packing case, and all the researchers in the Beijing Police Bureau and Ministry of Public Security who had spent most of their waking life during the Cultural Revolution working meticulously on these files were told to stop their work and pack up their files in preparation for their removal from Beijing. From the Beijing Railway Station, the files were to be transported out to Sichuan Province for long-term storage, and in that remote location, like the victims of the files themselves, they would disappear forever from public view. As the files left police headquarters at the beginning of their long journey to the west, so too did Liu and his fellow file workers depart from the ministry and return to normal police work.

The banishment of the personnel records of those purged during the Cultural Revolution might well be thought to constitute the end of the era of rule by file. Yet to think that would be to seriously underestimate the power of the record in China.

When Liu left police headquarters and returned to normal police duties, his life would again be dominated by the task of maintaining and checking records. This time, however, the focus of his work would shift away from the files of the elite and to the registers of those on the street.

"You have to understand that policing at this time was not law enforcement, for there was no law," Liu explains in describing his early days on the beat on the streets of Jiaodaokou.[5] "Politics ruled then, and the political line we were to adopt came to us via internal regulations." It was from these internal regulations that Liu learned the art of grassroots policing. "You have to remember," he explains, "that when I first arrived in Jiaodaokou, I'd come from the army and didn't really understand much about public security work. So older police comrades taught me about police work while I was out there working on the job." He continues, "I learned to first seek out the [political] activists and local revolutionaries in the community and then to get them to finger the five reactionary 'black' categories I was supposed to keep an eye on.[6] You have to remember," he repeats, "that there were no laws at this time, only regulations." Then, as an afterthought he adds, "and of all the regulations we were called upon to implement it was the record of households, the so-called household register, that was easily the most important to us."

Liu's afterthought reminds us once again of the centrality of records in China, although now he is talking about the records of ordinary residents rather than those of the powerful and famous.

Indeed, as Liu makes clear, records were easily the most crucial resource in understanding the dynamics of neighborhood politics and society in urban China during and even after the years of revolutionary activity. The importance of these everyday records of households was heightened by the adoption of the First Five-Year Plan in 1953. The registration of households and the details they carried within them of their occupants was critical, not only for policing but also for economic planning. The registers gave central planners an overview of the nation's human resources and their location across the whole of China. Indeed, the importance of the register to social stability and cohesion was underlined by the revolution itself.

As poor, displaced peasants' and workers' families fleeing the perils of the civil war came into Beijing in search of sanctuary, they were allocated work by the Communists, and it was their new workplaces that set about allocating them housing close to their places of employment. Old inner-city suburbs like Jiaodaokou started to fill up and change as ever more people arrived. With little money to spare for housing, local authorities appropriated and "renovated" the old dynastic courtyard-style households of the wealthy. As these households were "proletarianized," the Confucian ideal of four generations under one roof gave way to a new spatial arrangement that enabled dozens of families to live in the one compound house. Under the new regime the finely tuned symbolic structure of the traditional compound house was replaced by a series of ramshackle structures that filled in the central courtyard areas and in some cases housed scores of poor families. It was these new households that the Communists needed to understand if their rule was to survive and prosper.

As a result, when the First Five-Year Plan swung into operation in 1953, so, too, did household registration. In that year the Ministry of Public Security announced the first national registration of households. Once registration was complete, internal migration came to an end, and communities stabilized around workplaces. From this time onward, every resident was registered to a household and every household tied to a workplace. The registers of households, however, were under the control of the local community household registration police. Thus the register not only helped planners identify where human resources were located; it also helped police know where everyone lived and what their class background was. Indeed, the register became the key mechanism by which police came to know the daily lives of the ordinary people under their jurisdiction. To know an area meant knowing the record, and this, more than anything else, became the central component of all community police work.

"At this time," says Liu, "we needed to be on top of the 'four knows.' That is to say, we needed to know every individual's name, surname, address, and class background throughout our jurisdictional area. The police chief would periodically test us on our knowledge of our area by grabbing the register, calling out a name, and asking us where that person lived. He then checked our responses against the record. So the police station constantly practiced these sorts of tests. We were tested like this all the time."

With thirty years of revolutionary experience chiefly in Beijing and its suburbs, Liu passed all these tests. Indeed, he not only knew all the people in his neighborhood; he even knew the number of windows they had in their house and how much money each of them was being paid. Such an intimate knowledge of the neighborhood and its residents' lives was possible because, by the end of the 1950s, these areas had solidified into very tight, closed, and stable communities. The transformation of neighborhoods into communities was reinforced by the fact that all housing stock had been nationalized and was under the control of workplaces, which had assumed responsibility for housing their employees. Under these conditions China was not only the land of the register, but also the land of the work-unit system.[7]

The work-unit system was built around one's place of employment. The work unit was the first brick in a structure that offered a radically different mode of life from the one that prevailed in the West. Increasingly, work units weren't just places of employment; they also provided housing for their employees, childcare and schooling for the employees' children, clinics and hospitals for their family when they became sick, entertainment centers for when they had leisure time, and shops for when they needed to buy all of life's basic necessities. As work units set about building the infrastructure of these little communities, the whole concept of the city began to change.

Whereas Western cities often grew in concentric circles around a central business district or shopping precinct, in the New China cities took on an altogether different shape. The concept of the central business district all but disappeared as smaller, often discrete workplace-based industrial villages grew, and it was around these that all life began to revolve. These supplied their worker-residents with all their needs but simultaneously tied them to their places of employment by a very strict system of household registration that fixed them for life to their registered workplace address.

"In fact," says Liu, "if you wanted to enter or leave Beijing, in those days you would first need to get the approval of the local work-unit Party secretary. Without that, you couldn't even buy a train ticket, much less go anywhere!"

As a result of these tight restrictions, China not only established new types of socialist cities but also, unintentionally, reintroduced a very old form of sociability based on a very different understanding of the way an economy works. Indeed, work units were much more than economic units, becoming home, provider, benefactor, and, ultimately, one's claim to a certain personal status.

Essentially, work units operated less along modern notional economic lines than on the basis of what the ancient Greeks called an *oikonomos*, a word whose central component is the *oikos*, house(hold). Whereas in ancient Greece daily household life was dominated by patriarchy, in the New China's work units, it was dominated by politics. In effect, work units established a political economy tying together economic, moral, juridical, and ethical concerns all operating under a system of "favors" distributed on the basis of political assessments. The dominance of politics was further reinforced by the more restricted use of money, which from 1955 on was effectively devalued because of the introduction of ration coupons. From that time onward, the purchase of any significant item required money plus work-unit-distributed ration coupons. This arrangement, coupled with the suppression of wage differentials, led to the return of a very different kind of currency, one based on affective comradely relationships. "The work unit became like one's parents and one's family," says the writer Yi Zhongtian. It was the place where one was no longer friendless or wretched, adds the social scientist He Xinghan; and in the view of possibly China's foremost critic of the work unit, Lu Feng, the work unit was a place that, over time, transformed socialist relations into a form that looked remarkably like a lineage or clan relation.[8]

With work units allocating, not selling, housing and luxuries attainable only by combining money with work-unit-allocated ration coupons, money was no longer the universal translator, and benefits were obtainable only within a very particular and peculiar economy of "favors" centered around one's political performance and class background. The more politically active one was, the more likely that person was to receive favors from his or her work unit. This highly politicized economy became central not only to one's sense of self, but also to one's social standing. Chinese call this complex and affective linkage *guanxi*, connectedness. It produced a mode of life that, in an altogether different context, was famously referred to by the French anthropologist Marcel Mauss as a "gift economy."

Gift economies, says Mauss, work on three interrelated obligations, namely the obligations to give, to receive, and, perhaps most important, to reciprocate. These obligations are not codified but remain public secrets. Everyone obeys these rules, but no one acknowledges them as rules per se. Mauss was insistent that this system makes a gift economy almost the antithesis of the alienated transactions of economics. Instead of "clean," personality- and affect-free, economic transactions, the gift economy constructs an emotional relation that results in economic, moral, juridical, aesthetic, and mythological relations all being tied together. Indeed, a gift economy overshoots the restricted idea of economics so much that Mauss acknowledges that gift-based relations lead to a "system of total services."[9]

The giving of gifts is also based on a very different premise from that of straightforward economics. Giving a gift builds an emotional connection with the recipient that is inherently opaque, lacks any connotation of self-interest, and is incalculable. The emotional connectivity established in these systems stems, according to Mauss, from the fact that any actual "present" being given is always secondary to the human bond that the actual act of giving created. In other words, it is the thought that counts. Far from becoming mere business partners, then, gift partners become friends, family, or, in the highly politicized case of China, comrades. This is because, as Mauss would have it, "to make a gift of something to someone is to make a present of some part of oneself," while to receive a gift is to "accept some part of [another's] spiritual essence, of his soul."[10]

There is, then, in the gift economy, a merging of people and things.[11] One continues to give, as part of an ongoing psychic need to pay back a debt, and the greater the sense of indebtedness—be it toward gods or toward a political party—the more burdened one is by this psychological need to repay. In this system of understanding, then, the initial gift is always the crucial gift, for every subsequent countergift must always be in excess of the one originally given. Given the power of the work unit to define self and society in the China of the 1950s, the dynamics of social relations become all too clear.

With the original Party gift being "liberation," work units became both the sites where the Party would convert this abstract notion into a concrete material form (housing, school, hospitals, cinemas, and so forth) and the places where people could express their thanks concretely by participating in work-unit-based political campaigns or local mass-line organizations. Therefore, on the whole and in the main, people of the work unit enthusiastically took up the Party call. Throughout these revolutionary years, however crazy the scheme or radical the call, there were always activists who were ready, willing, and able to paint their part of town red. People were willing to participate in every one of the Party's political campaigns, not because they were forced to join in or even because they feared what would happen to them if they did not. Certainly, fear and perceived potential coercion were never absent from such campaigns, but people saw participation as a way of discharging their genuine sense of indebtedness. This dynamic would remain in place right up until the mid-1970s, when political exhaustion and alienation in the closing hours of the Cultural Revolution reduced the gift economy to a form of self-interested favors.

The significance of people's sense of their indebtedness to the Party is evidenced by what Liu tells us in passing about his experience with activists during the Cultural Revolution in Jiaodaokou: "You have to understand that in the old days, during the Cultural Revolution, if you needed an activist to help you do something, like

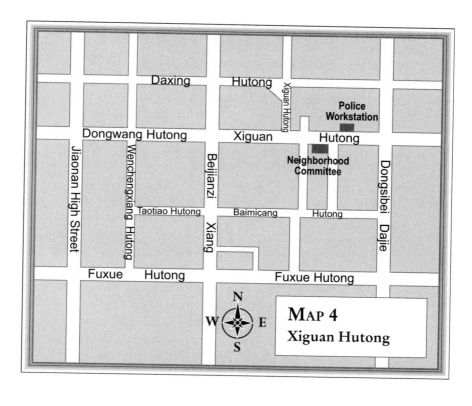

MAP 4

Xiguan Hutong

get involved in security patrols, they would always willingly do so and do so with alacrity. In those days, there were so many street-level activists that if someone wasn't asked, they would actually get very offended. So when we, say, formed a security patrol, if we didn't invite someone to join in, they would get really upset. Why? Well, that was because not to be invited was kind of insulting. The person concerned felt unwanted, unloved, and unnecessary. Such people would also get really nervous because they thought that we looked down on them, that we thought they had some sort of a political problem, that they weren't really good enough . . . that they were bad people . . . In the past that was the basic attitude of pretty much every political activist. Under these conditions you certainly didn't need to offer them money to do things. On the contrary, if you offered money they'd probably swear and spit in your face. What an insult, as though they were doing this just for the money! They wouldn't take a cent from you, because they didn't look at this job as work but as part of their political duty."

While Liu helps us to understand the concrete effects of this gift of politics upon activists, it is the stories told to us by the little old ladies of the neighborhood committees whom we meet on our sojourns through the back streets of Jiaodaokou that help us understand their personal burden of debt more clearly. As we leave the Yuan'en Temple area and cut across the busy South Jiaodaokou Boulevard and into another community known as the Xiguan Lane area, we are, in effect, leaving one version of "old Beijing" only to return to another.

In Xiguan Lane we find an area where no tourist tricycles venture and where few tourists ever go. Here is Jiaodaokou without the hype, without the restoration work, and without the coffee shops and fancy public toilets. In these dirty, smelly, rundown back streets we encounter a group of old ladies who make up this area's neighborhood security committee and who tell us of an old Beijing

36   Zhang Shuyin (right), the oldest member of the Xiguan Lane neighborhood committee.

very different from the restored Disneyland version across the road in the Yuan'en Temple area.

Wandering along the streets and alleyways, checking on security doors and the locks on houses and bicycles, are the little-old-lady patrols of Xiguan Lane. We come across them on the steps of an entrance to a compound house where they have stopped to catch their breath and replenish their refreshments. The twinkle in the eyes of the oldest among them catches our attention.

Her name is Zhang Shuyin, and she is ninety-three years old. Half blind, arthritic, partly deaf, and without teeth, she hardly seems a model of professional policing, yet there is something about her that speaks of a strong determination to do her bit. As we sit down to share our words and worlds, Zhang tells us in an almost impenetrable Shanxi accent how as a peasant girl she made her way to this city half a century ago. As she does so, the twinkle in her eyes turns into tears.

"I came here in '47, with my husband," she says, recalling the bad old days of civil war. "We came here on foot, can you believe it, on foot, all the way from Shanxi! We had to; there was no choice. So we tried our luck on the road." This was a walk of about 300 miles. It was no Jack Kerouac trip of self-discovery. This was a journey for survival. "If we had stayed, we would have starved," she says. "We had been farmers until the civil war came and destroyed most of our farm. If that wasn't bad enough, '46–'47 was also the time of a very bad harvest. So our crops failed, and what little else we had was lost in the war. We were left with nothing . . . nothing even to eat." She pauses as she wipes away another tear of remembrance. "You would not believe the way we suffered, back then . . . what they did to us . . . to me . . . but I can't talk about that," she sobs, "I just can't . . . it was just so terrible, so dark and so unspeakable."

Thus begins a tale of almost biblical proportions. Zhang Shuyin and her husband walked for forty days and nights. By the time they reached Beijing, they had barely enough in their stomachs to keep them alive. "We had nothing, absolutely nothing . . . just the rags on our backs. You have no idea what it was like back then . . . no idea. We had to beg our way to Beijing . . . begging for just a single cup of water, begging, just for the cast-off scraps of food from other people's tables and bins. It was awful. By the time we got here, we were half-naked and three-quarters dead. We had originally thought about going to Tianjin because my husband had a cousin there, but there was nothing there for us. So we struggled to Beijing instead."

Now installed in the compound house at 19 Xiguan Lane, Mrs. Zhang sits out her twilight years in the company of other old women who make up the bulk of the neighborhood security committee. As she looks at her friends while reflecting on those hard times, her mood brightens. "You know, life was really hard back then. We always ate poorly and never had enough to eat. We would eat anything, and I ate just to stop the feeling of hunger from overwhelming me. It's funny, you know, but back then when I was young and healthy I never had enough to eat. Now I'm old and crippled, and I've got more than enough to eat, but, these days, I don't have enough teeth left to eat with!" She chuckles to herself as she says this. Breaking free of the memories of remorseless poverty that overcame her, she resumes a warmer note and a wry smile.

At this point her closest friend and neighbor, the sprightly seventy-five-year-old Jiang Kuaijung, pops her head through the gateway door to see what all the noise is about. As she does, she is already joining in the conversation. "C'mon, Shuyin, we mightn't have had a lot to eat, but at least we shared what we had back in the old days." She, too, has a harrowing tale to tell of life before liberation.

Jiang had been eight years old when she was enslaved in a Japanese factory in Manchuria. Eventually she managed to escape and finally, after many hardships, landed in Jiaodaokou. Unlike Zhang, however, her story focuses not on suffering but on salvation.

37   Photos of Hu Zhuyun and her colleague appear on
      every notice board in the Xiguan Lane area.

"I can remember living here in the earlier period and getting home late from work, and my neighbors would rush over with some food for me to eat. We all ate together a lot back then, and although we have more now than we did back then, no one shares things anymore. Everybody is out for themselves these days, but you know, it really wasn't like that back in the old days. In fact, in those days it wasn't even necessary to lock your gates. These days we can't even leave home without locking everything up. That is why we have had to start this campaign for 'security courtyards' [an'quanyuan]," she says as she bangs on one of the ugly new gray security gates that are ubiquitous in this area of Jiaodaokou. Security, not socialism, it seems, is the new campaign slogan in this part of Jiaodaokou.

At this moment the policewoman in charge of the Xiguan area appears, sauntering slowly down the alleyway. We recognize her not only because of her uniform but also because we have seen her face many times before; in this part of town it appears on every notice board in every compound household entrance. Detailing her phone numbers, her office hours, and the police substation's address, her little sign is as ubiquitous in Xiguan Lane as the commercial advertisements are over in Yuan'en Temple area. Now we have a chance to see the residents' reaction to her. It comes as something of a surprise.

"Read any human-rights report on China and sooner or later you'll see the word 'policeman' coupled with words such as 'torture' or 'brutality,'" Carole Cadwalladr has written recently.[12] Yet here we are, in a Beijing backstreet, sitting with a group of old ladies who react to the appearance of this policewoman as though they are greeting a long-lost daughter. Cadwalladr has a point. Nevertheless, in China, policing beyond the law doesn't always mean overstepping one's authority. In the Xiguan Lane area, at least, it seems also to involve going beyond official duties to make sure that a community is well looked after. If gift economies

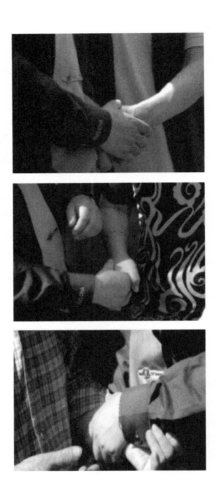

38   Greetings between policewoman
Hu and Xiguan Lane residents have
an affectionate tactile quality.

overstep the limits and laws of economics, Hu Zhuyun similarly oversteps the law-enforcement role of a policewoman. Part policewoman, part social worker, part friend, part daughter, Hu Zhuyun clearly has multiple roles in Xiguan Lane.

"Little Hu," "little Hu," "Hu Zhuyun," yell the old ladies as the policewoman strolls in our direction. "You've got to meet our younger sister Hu," they insist to us excitedly. Down the alleyway she comes, flashing a warm smile. As she saunters over and joins our conversation, we are struck by the old women's clear affection, attested by their use of the intimate language of family.

There is a tactile quality to their greetings, and words like *ganqing* (emotional connection), *renqing* (human feelings), and *guanxi* pepper their conversation. Clearly, these residents' relationship with this face of authority is an affective not a bureaucratic one. It may still turn upon the gift, but the basis of the gift seems to have metamorphosed from politics into friendship.

"We were just telling our new friends here that we are conducting a security campaign," says Jiang, obviously keen to please young Hu. Turning to us, she adds, "Young Sister Hu here is in charge of that campaign. She's our leader!" Hu deflects the compliment with a shake of her hand and mutters under her breath, "We are all in this together," but her beaming smile betrays her pleasure in the accolade. Whether out of embarrassment or concern, she quickly changes the conversation and begins asking them about their families, their illnesses, their homes, their children, and their grandchildren. In the process she reveals an intimacy with their lives that suggests that the community police still know everything about their residents just as they did in the days when Liu was being tested by the police chief.

"She gave us these," says one of the old women, pulling out from under her tunic a card containing Hu's name, telephone number, address, and photograph. "She told us to wear these dog tags just in case we get lost. That way, if we are in another part of the city and get lost or a little disoriented, she can always be contacted." All the women start pulling out their dog tags and wiggle them in front of us. "She is in charge of *our* security," Jiang says, laughing at her clever play on her own words. Hu adds a note of seriousness to the frivolity.

"It's true," says Hu, "I'm in charge of security in this community [*shequ*], but you know, in the Chinese tradition, being responsible for security basically means that any problem that pops up is one that I have to deal with. That means getting involved in all sorts of things that aren't strictly policing. In fact, I'm often more like a social worker than a cop," she says with a smile.

Indeed she is. Hu will help the homeless find cheap rental accommodation, help arguing couples sort out their marriage problems, help migrants sort out registration problems, and help the local unemployed or recently released criminals find work. She even arranges get-togethers for those who cannot get out to the New Year festivities. "I get them all together for a traditional meal of Chinese dumplings. In Chinese, we call them *jiaozi*. Do you know them? You wrap meat in pastry . . . Well, while the woman chat and make the *jiaozi*, the men go off on a security patrol of the neighborhood."

Even when she talks more about her role as the community police officer of the area, security is never far from her thoughts. "Have you checked on the doors and locks this morning?" she asks the old ladies from the security committee. They nod, assuring her that everything is in order. She then turns to us and invites us to join her on patrol.

So we bid farewell to Zhang, Jiang, and their companions and join Hu on her daily rounds. As we make our way through this labyrinth of *hutongs,* she explains the Xitong Lane area. "There are six alleyways and eight main streets that make up this community," she says. Involving a population of around 4,700 people, 568 of whom are migrants, living in a total of 260 rooms, Hu's work is

39   Hu sells the value of security doors in Xiguan Lane.

far from easy, as each of these households must be registered. This, along with the maintenance of the register for shops and markets, is no small task. Yet, as she points out, this is not her main task at the moment. "The main thing I do at the minute is try to convince everyone in the compound households of the need to replace their old rickety gateways with stronger security doors."

Along with her volunteer security staff, Hu is selling the value of security doors like a Mormon missionary selling Jesus. The results, she says, have been pleasing. Of the 176 occupied compounds, about 62 have now earned the designation "security courtyards." This means that their gates are secure, that each dwelling has good locks on all doors and windows, that a system of "neighborhood watch" is in place within the compounds, and that each compound has a responsible person in charge of courtyard security.

"We cannot force people to adopt the 'secure courtyard strategy,' for this they must do themselves. We can't pay for the locks and security doors because, ultimately, that is the residents' responsibility," she says. Nevertheless, her job is to persuade all of them to "trade money for security" (hua qian mai ping'an), and although some aren't keen and have to be convinced, few openly oppose her scheme. "The key thing," she says, "is to try to win their confidence," and Hu, it seems, is an expert at that. Just how expert becomes evident as we meander through the alleyways.

As we pass one compound, a resident from within spots Hu and comes rushing out to greet her. She tells us that she's proud of her, and immediately begins to hold her hand, saying, "She really looks after the people around here." Pointing to the ugly gray security door on the front of her compound courtyard, she says, "And this is her success story." The woman then explains. "You have to remember that in China, you don't have insurance companies to provide any 'incentive' to get people to invest in their own security. In China, that all has to be done by persuasion. Most community police are men, but Sister Hu is a woman!" she says, giving Hu a

40   The chipped, chiseled, faded slogan on this spirit wall might
      once have read something like "Long live Chairman Mao,
      long live the Communist Party, and long live China."

thumbs-up. As we move on to other *hutongs* and other courtyards, the same scene is repeated wherever we go.

As we enter another compound, the faded remnants of the Maoist past greet us on the spirit wall just inside the entranceway. Chipped, chiseled, and faded beyond recognition, it might once have read something like "Long live Chairman Mao, long live the Communist Party, and long live China." These days, it's just a faded white wall in need of repair. Indeed, in this part of town, it is as though politics have become as faded as the wall itself. Yet despite this we still find, in the behavior of these older residents at least, the telltale signs of an enduring "gift." Let us call it the gift of comradeship, even though these days it is usually spoken of under the code of friendship or family. As we look at this wall and try to read the now undecipherable characters, one of the residents comes out of her house and hugs Hu, then drags her past the spirit wall and into the compound. As we follow Hu, she begins to make idle conversation with yet another old woman.

"How's life?" she asks as she admires the flowers that sit on the old woman's windowsill. "Life's just fine," says the old lady with a huge grin. Hu smiles at her before turning to us and, while wagging her finger at the old lady, says, in mock seriousness, "You know, this is one lucky old lady; her son is so *xiaoshun* [filial and obedient]. And her grandson, well, he's now in college learning design, isn't that right?" The old lady beams with pride as she nods in agreement. She then tells Hu about the gift she has just received from the young college boy. "He's just a poor student, yet he has still managed to buy his old grandmother a pair of gold bracelets. Imagine that! They are so valuable I dare not wear them outside the compound!" she says. "Keep them in a safe place, then," says Hu, as she disentangles herself from the tactile old lady and makes her way out the door. "Don't bother seeing us out," says Hu as the old lady follows us out. "Don't bother following us," says Hu as the old lady follows us to the end of her street.

"Ordinary people around here have more of a feeling for their community than residents in many other areas," says Hu, trying to explain the generosity of spirit that seems to greet her every move. "Sure, the mass line is harder to enforce these days than it was in the past, but here, there is still a feeling of community that you don't get elsewhere." At one corner we see a big red banner across the alleyway proclaiming: "Big families and small families all rely upon the masses." Here, in Xiguan Lane area at least, this slogan from the Maoist past still seems to hold true, in a way. Here, in Xiguan Lane, we still find a reliance on the masses, and in many ways this makes Xiguan Lane something of a living relic of a bygone era. Yet it is also a very new form of living rather than a mere vestige; a post-Maoism, if you like. Here, in Xiguan Lane, we find a Maoism without the politics, without the violence, and without the roar of the crowd. It lives the dream of comradeliness not as political solidarity but as a return to the collectivist spirit that Maoism once tapped into and that China has not yet fully exhausted. Here, then, is a different temporality, a meandering tributary, a slow-flowing stream destined to join the headlong rush to modernity that is Beijing. It is but one suburb of this city . . . And now it's time to move on, to another.

4 ETERNAL RETURN

If time is infinite but matter limited, all events can be assumed to recur eternally, Nietzsche once told us. Yet when the eternal hourglass is turned, can we so readily assume that all the grains will always fall in exactly the same place? Historical forms might very well be recycled and fall like grains of sand, but do they ever simply fall into the same place; do they ever return as pure repetition? Once as tragedy, then as farce, said Marx. Eternal return, perhaps, but maybe it comes in a form that is not immediately recognizable. Maybe it reappears as a grotesque form of realism or as an aestheticized politics. Maybe it returns as a latent rather than explicit manifestation. It might take the appearance of the new, but, at a latent level, is it not always the same, as both Walter Benjamin and Theodor Adorno said of the commodity? Can we not see it in the way Tiananmen Square unconsciously connected to ancient architectonic forms, or the way the city axis was turned rather than overturned? Manifest only in their latency, modern signs of power such as technology—be it the British with the East Zhengyangmen Railway Station or the Maoists and post-Maoists with their subways and freeways—use ancient forms of power, such as the cosmology of Beijing's fortified city walls, as their foundation. Can we not see it also in the way latent community attitudes and habitual forms reappeared only to be reconfigured in forms that either spoke to the politics of the moment or, in more muted forms, learned to live in a new economy of meaning? To continue to live out the gift in a world where everything around one is being commodified—is this not a sign of an eternal return? Much of what was once manifest might appear ephemerally in the new. The dustbin of history, then, always has its ragpickers and recyclers. They will forage through this historical debris, searching for the eternal, lifting out those things that can be "turned," transformed and reconfigured. This task is as important for those with a will to power as it is for the ragpicker. Like a ragpicker of time, we, too, have been sifting through this dustbin of history trying to identify, sort

41   Cycle, recycle: the eternal return.

through, and order the trash, trying to find what can be extracted, what has been recycled, and what is left once the transformation takes place.

Rubbish tells us a lot about a city, not only about the scale and tempo of changes taking place, but also about its fashions and excesses as they are endlessly remade and recycled. Rubbish, therefore, tells us about the cyclical nature of time, about its collection, disposal, and, above all, its recycled nature. For a place like Beijing, where time is linear and progress is unquestioned, the eternal return is itself a dirty word, an irreversible curse. So it seems somehow appropriate to look for an alternative to this linear time in that place of dirt and grime, the rubbish dump.

There is a village on the outskirts of Beijing, a place that no taxi driver knows and to which few will venture. It is off the city map and out of time. It is, in some crucial ways, an eternal return. Every morning the ragpickers go off to work on their tricycles to collect rubbish, and every evening they return. It is an eternal process out of kilter with a full sense of Beijing time.

At one level, this village is gripped by the same endless rush forward that characterizes Beijing time. It is where the huge piles of the past (and things that package the new) are discarded as rubbish as Beijingers pursue a bright new modernist future. Yet it is also the place where the ragpicker collects, sorts, and recycles that rubbish in an endless process that resembles an eternal return. This netherworld of development, neither thrusting forward nor fully "returning," is called Bajiacun.

It is here, in Bajiacun, amid the dust and debris of a city's refuse, that the moments and memories of the city are picked through, sorted, taken, and then reprocessed in order to ensure that the "real" Beijing time is not choked by its own excess or reminded of its own many cycles.

In so many ways, time carries no profundity in a place that lives off recycled matter. Traces of time slipping away can be discerned

42   The moments and memories of the city are
picked through, sorted, and reprocessed.

only from the decay of objects and from the graying hair and wrinkled faces of the ragpickers themselves. The timepiece outside the National Museum in Tiananmen Square that counted down the days to the 1997 Hong Kong handover and now counts down the number of days until the 2008 Olympics means little to the people of Bajiacun. These events don't change their worldview or their sense of self as Chinese. They do not live their Chineseness monumentally, as Tiananmen would want them to do. Instead, and despite the squalor, there is a settledness in their attitudes just as there is harmony in their recycled time. This harmonic balance is all too absent from Beijing time. Thus, while the city runs full throttle and rebuilds itself into an Olympic showplace, Bajiacun runs cyclically, in a way that is perhaps more in keeping with the traditional Chinese sense of temporality than a positivist dream of modernity. Every dump is essentially the same, yet in each there are traces and traits that make it distinctive. For migrant workers in the recycling town of Bajiacun, eternity returns every day as sheer remorseless grind, dirt, and squalor. Weighed down by exploitative contracts, long hours, and hard toil, ragpickers are caught in a life amid the dirt. And yet this dirt is a carnival of color.

As scavenging birds circle in the sky above, the ragpickers of Bajiacun have already landed. On the ground, people move about groundlessly. Try sitting on the pavement and observing these people: the motion of cycling and recycling dazzles and whirls you away from your initial gaze. You are lost in dreams or an uncertain future, but then so, too, is this city.

On the endless construction sites throughout Beijing, contract laborers are digging themselves out of poverty as they sweep away the past. The imperial red grandeur of the Forbidden City is enclosed by the sprawling, gray monstropolis of a new Beijing. There is a woman cleaning the street in an orange jumpsuit who

43   A woman cleaning the street in an orange jumpsuit.

looks as if she has jumped straight out of Guantánamo Bay. No leg irons and handcuffs on her, only a broom and cart.

People on the ground move about in a haze of cigarette smoke, excessive amounts of carbon dioxide, and a perpetual cloud of dust that never seems to touch the ground. The high-rise buildings, low-key *hutongs,* the sky, and the ground all come together to form a city of seamless gray.

Gray is the color once imposed upon the common folk by imperial edict. Now it dominates again, but this time it is at the dictate of car exhaust fumes. The roadside trees are on the verge of choking, but still they give shade to locals who appear oblivious to the smoggy swirl and noxious fumes. There is money to be had in this gray, and there is no time to worry about the damage it might cause. It's another Great Leap, but this time Beijing is jumping in a very different direction. Mao would turn in his grave if he had one to turn in. Instead his recycled corpse lies rotting in a crystal sarcophagus in the middle of Tiananmen Square. The placement of his body in the middle of the square, once considered a sign of ultimate respect, is now often regarded as an embarrassment that haunts the present and blocks the ancient flow of masculine energy and spirit.

A new Beijing is in the making. After the Communist Revolution, the Great Leap, the Cultural Revolution, the Tiananmen Square Incident, and the marketization of the 1990s, the countdown to the 2008 Olympic Games is producing a renewed national pride and is subjecting Beijing to yet another facelift. Nearly every city resident can feel it. New roads and buildings are going up at a phenomenal speed while old, rundown houses are being demolished even more quickly. Restaurants and bars have sprung up in the east, north, and northwest—areas where foreigners and Chinese nouveau riche congregate, consume, spend, and enjoy themselves. The influx of *waidiren* (outsiders) to take jobs—from low-paid construction workers to high-profile bureaucrats—makes

44   The ragpickers whirl past in endless motion.

the self-proclaimed Beijingers appear as a minority in their own city. Under a typical Beijing sky, which is a depressing mix of black and white, the gray on the horizon looks more boundless and malleable than ever before.

Around 20,000 refuse collectors ride their tricycle carts into the city of Beijing to do their daily business. Some of them head southwest to nearby Zhongguancun, also known as the Silicon Valley of China; some strike east, to the burgeoning satellite suburb of Yayuncun, the newly defined 2008 Olympics business district; others venture farther into the city. Bajiacun is a world away from this Beijing. With listless and weathered faces, the Bajiacun ragpickers pedal around town in business suits. With their slightly underweight bodies, their drab and grimy suits, they present a parody of the successful besuited businessmen who watch them from their Audis. Indeed, twenty years earlier, the observers could very well have been those observed.

From the rear, this traffic looks like a peasant army on bicycles, tricycles, mopeds, and foot, swirling past us in the dust. From the front and in the eyes of the Beijing urbanites, it is more like a full-scale invasion. Once upon a time there was a very strict household registration system that kept this army at bay and on the farm. Now, with economic reform and the near collapse of the household registration system, nothing stops them. Indeed, the morning exodus from Bajiacun into the city is a metaphor for the mass exodus of all Chinese peasants from the countryside into the metropolis. That is the other side of contemporary Beijing.

Bajiacun is part of the Chinese capital even though no one wants to recognize it as such. Just outside the fourth ring road, this shantytown is nothing like the rest of the city but forms an independent kingdom heaped with urban material relics. It's off the tourist map, rarely gets policed, and goes unacknowledged by most Beijingers, yet it is well known to most Chinese migrant workers.

On their way out to work every day, the temporary resident-workers of Bajiacun are reminded by the red banners flanking the roadside to "speak standard Mandarin." To work in Georges Bataille's homogeneous world, the ragpickers of Bajiacun must assimilate. As the sun climbs farther from the horizon, the heat intensifies, warming up the vast rubbish tips on both sides of Shuangqing Road. A new stench arises to greet the next floating populace of Bajiacun.

By nine in the morning the chaos of traffic departing for Beijing has abated and the haze of dust has begun to settle. As the smog lifts like a curtain it reveals, as if by magic, a different street scene. Appearing as if from nowhere are the "mobile" street workers of Bajiacun itself. Bike repairers, metal welders, flea marketers, vegetable sellers, and snack vendors now dominate and transform the streets. People—mostly men—start appearing on the sidewalks. Wearing poor-quality suits and black leather shoes, they look as if they are on their way to a construction site. Meanwhile young women wearing scanty, cheap tank tops and miniskirts or long satin nightgowns peek out from hairdressing salons. The morning scenes of Bajiacun present a parody of the nightlife found in central Beijing. Indeed, Bajiacun itself appears to be little more than a grotesque, inverted rendition of the glimmering city to the south. Yet Bajiacun offers an uncanny re-rendering. Here the rush to modernize and advance takes the form of dirt and grime, and development appears, paradoxically, as a snapshot of underdevelopment. The smoke and undifferentiated clutter of Bajiacun are like excremental waste, creating a horrifying feeling of déjà vu that Beijing is desperately seeking to hide and forget. Shit might disturb, but it also vitalizes the modernization that Beijing has so passionately embraced. Behind the idle shopfronts on both sides of Bajiacun's streets there is a world of abundance, color, and vibrancy.

Yet it is a world turned on its head. The city has shopping malls; the courtyards of Bajiacun are rubbish malls. Beijing's malls offer a variety of new specialty goods; Bajiacun's courtyards offer a

45   A Bajiacun rubbish mall/recycling center.

46   A mountain of remaindered books rendered into strips.

variety of rubbish. The city has gleaming bookshops; Bajiacun's courtyards have mountains of remaindered books. The city has its high-rises; the ragpickers build skyscrapers of metallic rubbish. Point and counterpoint . . . Bajiacun is a grotesque, uncanny parody of the city itself.

From ten o'clock on, fully loaded tricycle carts come back to this inverted city in dribs and drabs. They enter the courtyard "shops" laden with a variety of domestic refuse. The individual collectors bring their rubbish to the trash dealers with whom they have established *guanxi*. The load on the cart has already been sorted into different categories—paper, plastic bags, wood, metal, rubber, and so on—and these will soon be further reclassified by the two or three ragpickers who work behind their bosses, who stand propped up against the all-important set of scales.

Mounds of classified garbage in the recycling center are gold mines to these dealers, processors, and ragpickers. For ragpickers like Li Ruide and his wife Huang from Henan, sorting different-quality plastic bags into piles in a tiny section of an outdoor recycling center in Beijing's trash town is an economically better option than working their own fields back home. For among so much rubbish—which will soon be sold in exchange for cash—ragpickers sometimes find preloved items that still work and are of use. The couple found Pokémon toys when every kid in the city had had one. Radios ended up as junk when mobile phones and iPods came into vogue. In early July, tons of books, especially textbooks, dominate the recycling center. Before Chinese New Year, a massive volume of old, dismantled furniture is seen across town. The couple explains the rubbish cycle to us in the same way farmers would explain crop rotation. More than a bumper crop in agriculture, mass production of garbage is a sign of vigorous capitalism. It implies an imbalance between desire and matter, an excess of consumption. Commodities in Beijing no longer enjoy longevity as they did in the old days. Expiration dates assign material products

47   Huang and Li.

life expectancy well before they fall into disuse. But pieces of junk often take on very different lives once they have been collected by the city recyclers. They travel and continue to exist in unintended shapes and forms way past their use-by dates. Their travel routes tell us tales of Beijing's development process, and their ownership reveals the complex sentiments of a very different point in time. Entering the recycling centers of Beijing, we learn of the fickleness of the city's fads and fancies as well as the nostalgia that makes people hold onto things.

Li and Huang came to Beijing eight months ago to seek better-paid jobs. Through a Henan contact here, they found a trader, also from Henan, who took them on as rubbish sorters. At a time when government reserves have reached a trillion U.S. dollars, they are paid a total of 600 yuan (75 U.S. dollars) a month; the trader provides housing accommodation. We wonder how long it will take them to save enough money to afford to buy their own house back home, since they say this is why they have come to Beijing.

Li and Huang live in a shabby three-square-meter dorm room in the compound at the back of the rubbish heap. To reach it, we trudge through greenish-gray mud and scraps of garbage; Li wades through the sludge barefoot, letting his trousers dip in the unknown mix. There has been frequent rain in Beijing as a result of government efforts to seed the clouds. It's a shame that these two are no longer farmers. They lead us into a flooded, rotting shack as cheerfully as they would have had they been back on their farm in Henan. We duck in the narrow walkway to avoid a line hung with a dazzling array of cheap damp clothes. At the very back of the compound is their one-room living space. Its furnishings consist of a shaky wooden single bed on which Li's wife sleeps, a couple of stools, and a hatstand decked out like a Christmas tree. An ample supply of Erguotou—cheap Chinese spirits particularly popular with the working class—stands in one corner. On one of the stools are a few packets of no-name-brand cigarettes. An aluminum bucket of dirty water stands amidst the mess of dirty laundry and trash on the floor. A screaming fan on the verge of disintegration plays the music of industry. Li's bamboo mattress is rolled up against one leg of the bed. They motion for us to sit on their bed, saying they are happy to stand. At one end of the bed is a boxy black radio covered in thick layers of dust and grime. Above the whine of the fan the radio's single speaker blasts out a tinny, flat, crackling government-sponsored national overview. Like all overviews, it blocks out the heterogeneity of lived experience. Its focus is well away from the smell, dirt, and toil of the ragpickers' lives.

The cacophony masks some secrets. While the radio blares, we look around the room. On the walls are dusty family photos next to decaying posters of medicine advertisements and a calendar from last year. If the same miscellaneous assortment were found in a Western house, it would perhaps be mistaken for fashionably bohemian retro. For the up-and-coming urbanites of Beijing, however, this miscellany of junk and smells adds up to a shithole.

The radio proclaims the centrality of Beijing time with the familiar beep marking the hour. Yet these people have not completely bought in to Beijing time. They are caught between two worlds, yet live in neither. In this ramshackle structure in a junk town, they sit on the edge of a progressive, modern, and go-ahead city. The radio announces Beijing time, but in this room there are no clocks. The ragpickers live a different time in Bajiacun. They live time as peasants do throughout China, by the moon and the sun. They rise at dawn every morning; as the sun sets, they have supper and go to bed. They fly a different flag of nation at Bajiacun, yet still they are connected to this city.

Li normally drinks himself to sleep, while Huang is too tired to do anything but go directly to sleep after a long hard day of labor. Their lifestyle is an eternal return, geared to an endlessly repeated daily cycle. Li and his wife work, eat, and sleep unaffected by government announcements about China's foreign reserves and by government efforts to cool down an overheated economy. For most sixty-year-olds, making a plan for retirement would be a wise thing to do, particularly in a country where life expectancy for males is seventy and for females seventy-three. "I have four children—two sons and two daughters. I don't want to depend on any of them," insists the thickly accented Li, whose stubborn attitude appears as unworldly as it is understandable.

It's a little hard to understand their move to Beijing. Li and Huang were happy in the countryside and didn't want to leave. Indeed, before coming here, they had never left their hometown, Kaifeng. Perhaps, as times got better year by year since Deng's inception of economic reform, Li saw some of his neighbors leaving home for the city and later returning with a lot of money. Over the past twenty years, some of his fellow townspeople must have managed to create visible wealth, their mud houses becoming first brick houses and then concrete ones. None of Li and Huang's children works the fields of wheat, cotton, and corn as their parents did; their eldest son is the chief of the village and their second son a taxi driver. Their daughters have married well; one of them works in a shoe factory in the southern city of Guangzhou. By Li's account, all his children have a reasonably good life with their new families. "I'm on the lookout for easy cash," says Li with admirable candor. But the same can be said of everyone else in China, and Li is on the bottom of the heap.

Streams of returning traffic flood back into Bajiacun after half-past three. Rubbish-adorned vehicles parade slowly along the main street like floats, a carnival of trash sporadically disrupted by gigantic honking trucks that swerve violently to overtake the languid wave of waste. For some collector-dealers, each truckload represents a whole day's work of gathering, sorting, and trading garbage from door to door. There is potential profit in that high stack of moldy, beaten-up mattresses, in those disentangled coils of wires securely fastened by strings. The dazzling array of rubbish will end up in the various backstreet recycling centers, making them look like highly decorated birthday cakes. Li and his wife have no time to chat in these peak afternoon hours. They must manually sort a profusion of plastic bags into whites, blacks, reds, grays, stripes, and so on. This harvest must be ready to be trucked away at five.

Five o'clock is the peak hour for the birds. Flocks of crows arrive in tight formation, land loudly crowing on the mountains of human waste while others remain in formation above, circling to ensure that the footsoldiers of their battalion are not left unprotected.

Meanwhile motor vehicles and tricycle carts continue to flood in, their loads gleaming in the golden twilight. A light wind blows the pungent odors from the recycling centers into the street. The smells of musty books, rusting scrap metal, rotting wood, and damp paper now combine with the more homely aromas of Xingjiang kebab, Shanxi sliced noodles, and northeastern spicy hot stew from the eateries on the pavements. Famous Beijing cuisine such as Peking duck and hot pot is unfamiliar to the Bajiacun workers. Out here it's hometown food they sell, and the sheer diversity of the restaurants gives some indication of where these people come from. But although these places tempt many passersby at this hour, for ragpickers like Li this is not yet the time to eat; the boss's trucks must be loaded after the sorting and sent off to the countryside before dusk. This is perhaps the busiest time of their day, and they won't eat until their employer has a cooked supper for them all once the trucks have been loaded.

Li and Huang work hurriedly amid the riot of variously colored plastic bags strewn about in their employer's small section of the recycling center. As if to offer living confirmation of the Sapir-Wharf hypothesis, Li names each and every type of plastic bag, just as Eskimos reportedly differentiate among sixteen types of snow. Even the smallest differences in quality and color need to be taken into account. Each type of plastic bag must then be put in its own bigger *hashen* bag. Making distinctions among them all is crucial to Li's job; any mistakes at this end will cost Li's boss at the other end. As the big trucks arrive to transport the bags to faraway Hebei, where a huge reprocessing plant awaits them, Li and his wife hurriedly finish their last few loads. Picking up plastic bags of the same type from the sea of PVC in front of them, they compress them to remove any lingering unprofitable pockets of air, then throw them into the *hashen*. Beads of perspiration cover Li's brow and drop onto the deflated bags. "Every grain of rice is a bead of sweat from a peasant's brow," claims a verse from a famous Tang poem. Here, Li and Huang harvest a very different crop: the shimmering drop commemorated in the Tang poem falls on a lifeless plastic bag.

As the warm summer evening deepens, we see some unfriendly-looking young girls strutting around in skimpy dresses. Unlike their Beijing-born coevals, their faces carry no trace of teenage innocence. Heavy, powdery-makeup masks hide their apprehension and insecurity in this world of the gutter. Their staggering steps betray their inexperience in the stiletto heels, or perhaps they are still intoxicated from a previous engagement. Cigarettes glow between their fingers. Their long hair is cheaply dyed. The smell of fake perfume on their bodies mingles with the body odors of their garbageman clients and the cheap cigarettes they both smoke. The dead river of Bajiacun does not stink at night. The half-moon is reflected crazily on the surface of the sludgy stream dotted with various floating rubbish stacks, their colors softened by the darkness and smoke. The moonlight on the puddles of sludge grotesquely evokes the legend about the death of the Tang poet Li Bai. Some of his most moving poems center on the romantic power of a full moon casting its light upon shimmering water. Li Bai is said to have drowned as he tried to catch the moon as it slipped into the waters beneath his feet. Li the ragpicker steps into the sludge puddles of Bajiacun every day, not because he wants to capture the moon, but because he wants to retrieve the plastic bags. Yet he, too, will die as a result. As one of the recycling bosses admits to us, "In Beijing, these country ragpickers survive from sorting trash, but they die from it, too. They live off the trash, but also die from the consequences."

For the ragpicker and the prostitute, life is really no life in Bajiacun.

Suddenly one of the girls turns away, shattering the Li Bai moment as she tosses a cigarette butt into the sludge puddle. She heads toward the massage parlor, where a man waits. The girl's eyes turn to meet the man's. A smile as fake as her hair suddenly covers her face. Fake perfume joins fake allure, but the client still looks happy. He immediately stands up, his eyes shine, and before a word is spoken, the man and the girl slip inside, becoming silhouettes behind a curtain.

Our thoughts return to Li and his wife in their damp, dark, little room behind the rubbish heap. By now he has probably got drunk and fallen half asleep smoking while the rhythm of the noisy little fan has helped Huang to fall into sleep. Another day of work is over. Tomorrow they will get up and repeat what they have done today, as they do every day. Do they dream of moonlit lakes or plastic bags?

Rubbish from Beijing sweeps through Bajiacun like plastic bags caught in the wind. From the trash city it is sold, sorted, and delivered to various processing plants in Henan and Hebei. The reprocessed materials are reused and reassembled, then make their way back to the city as new products. Shit and the sacred are tied together, for both offer the promise of ever-lasting life. If religion moves between the sacred and the profane, garbage moves between city and country. Reincarnation is guaranteed, because trash never dies. Bajiacun becomes its version of limbo.

Before getting into a cab and leaving the garbage behind, we take one last look at the trash city. The eternal return performed in Bajiacun merges with the star-filled sky to form a seamless picture.

Grotesque but poetic, it's an image of dirty romanticism. No sooner have we shut the door than the mirage vanishes as we, too, head off in a cloud of dust.

Rubbish abounds on every Beijing street, waiting to be discovered and purchased. Boutique shops along the dimmed, stylish street of Yandai Xiejie sell European and Japanese rejects and outmoded fashion items that are often purchased by those from the producing countries, if not by the hip, petit-bourgeois Chinese. Across town, in Wudaokou, less-well-off aspiring young rock musicians from China's northeast and northwest are wading through the ocean of saw-gash *(dakou)* CDs that are themselves becoming relics of Beijing cool. Outdoor music festivals in arid Lanzhou and the quaint southwestern town of Lijian resonate with the powerful underground force of Beijing's saw-gash generation *(dakou de yidai)*. The rebellious spirit from the "good old days" of Cui Jian (regarded as the father of China's rock and roll) still lingers on in post-Tiananmen Beijing, raised by the backstreet merchandising of dumped CDs from the West.

Trash becomes treasure in the hole-in-the-wall shops of the saw-gash generation, in the boutiques beside Shicha Lake, where commercial craft cruise. Recently arrived saw-gashed discs from the West are admired anew through the display windows of funky shops, while the previously popular imported discs are arranged in countless cardboard boxes outside shops for "panning" by curious passersby seeking to discover their own version of gold amidst the dross. The ceaseless return of these rejects as market items has made Beijing itself one big recycling center. The definition of waste is no longer clear. Smuggled garments with their labels ripped off become fashionable items and inspire China, the world's largest textile manufacturer, to invent more. CDs with a gash inspire sweet adolescent memories. People and stuff alike gather and overflow throughout the capital city, endlessly recycling themselves.

48   A saw-gash CD.

While Li pans for unexpected treasures in the trash of Bajia-cun, a bunch of kids in the university area of Wudaokou bury themselves in heaps of plastic, mining the rich reserves of gashed CDs to be found in dingy little shops. These CDs ushered in a unique Chinese subculture. But the kids of this generation are now witnessing, indeed participating in, the obsolescence of that sub-culture as they gradually abandon their saw-gash CDs in favor of Internet downloads.

In a backstreet shack in Wudaokou, Wang, twenty-six, is patiently looking through piles of gashed CDs in search of some Sex Pistols albums. The heyday of saw-gash CDs is over. Stricter dumping rules by record companies and the music-sharing net-works available via the web have made sure of that. Still, there are diehards like the amateur guitarist Wang. We meet him knee-deep in the chaos of illegal CDs just outside one of the few remaining CD shops in Wudaokou. These days, the saw-gash business depends on regulars like Wang, who have an idiosyncratic attachment to the disc. He tells us that although Internet downloads are the main source of his current collection, he still much prefers tripping off to CD shops like this. While he pans, he explains the excitement of chancing upon rare and excellent discs in a pile of rubbish CDs. "It's like winning the lottery," he says.

Faced with the decline of the saw-gash business from its heyday ten years ago, dealers have found a way to survive and thrive by combining sales of the remaindered CDs with those of pirated music and films on DVDs and videocassettes. Veteran saw-gash dealer Lin, twenty-four, foresees a future full of possibilities. After graduation from junior high school Lin came to Beijing, where he led a nomadic life, making friends with a few punk rockers, experimental musi-cians, self-proclaimed artists, and fellow wanderers. Through this circle he found a couple of contacts who enabled him to set up his business trading saw-gash CDs. Dealers like Lin hijacked the intended plastic rubbish, helping to create the significant youth culture known as the saw-gash generation, *dakou de yidai.*

The aspiring punk rock generation of Beijing didn't have the money to buy into that culture proper, but they could still dream, and they would link dreams of artistic freedom to the songs that came from damaged discs. A punk revolution grew not from themes of liberty offered in philosophical tomes but from Western castoffs. Playing these discs sold as rubbish was illegal in the West, a violation of copyight laws. In China the saw-gash trade influenced youth far more than decades of Cold War rhetoric, "polluting" Communist Party talk about a spiritual civilization, giving these rebels without a cause an antiauthority sense of direction. The abundance and cheapness of the dumped Western music "inspired a generation of kids to grow mohawks, wear leather, and pick up guitars."[1]

Perhaps the Beijing punks are more genuine than their Western counterparts. If punk culture is about pursuing greater individual freedom and not selling out to consumerism and mainstream interests, then "garbage" CDs offer an authentic alternative. Facing a real threat of arrest and imprisonment for their rebellious voices, the Beijing punks received their musical education from shiploads of "rubbish" sentenced to death overseas. Nevertheless, the spirit of resistance remained alive despite the forced closure of a number of punk-themed bars.

Such was the spirit of the saw-gash generation. Peaking just before 2000, the saw-gash kids bridged the gap between Beijing's "beat generation" and punk culture while adding a belated surprise element of their own. A vast array of cultural offshoots sprang up: websites, magazines, *dakou* music catalogs, *dakou* music critics, online forums, and *dakou* shopping guides. Saw-gash became more like a genre than a social ill. The significance and attractiveness of *dakou* lay in its "underground" character in a country with relatively strict censorship laws. For alternative-music fans, *dakou* music appeared as a previously hidden treasure, now suddenly both easily available and affordable. An unusually "filtered" selection of music from the West shaped not only the musical taste of those kids, but also their spirituality and perspective. You Dali, on a web discussion site, made a noteworthy observation:

> This is a *dakou* world, a new life where you don't even have to leave the country to realize your spiritual adventure. When Americans fiercely give themselves a cut, they also give the world a possibility of Communism and unity. The government doesn't encourage 1.3 billion people to listen to rock and roll. A small bunch of them therefore secretly look for offerings to their ears, to their eyes, to their brains, and to their generation . . . *Dakou* products have ushered 1 million Chinese youths into a new wave, a new listening sensibility, a new awareness, a new mindset, and a new set of values. Whether the *dakou* generation is a *jinkou* [import] generation or a *chukou* [export] generation confuses quite a few social observers.[2]

The throwaway societies of the West supplied a vast amount of musical nutrition and underground cultural vibe to a country in which youth culture had been largely absent. Indeed, the gash on the margin of the CDs—a visible sign of rejection—came to characterize a generation of Chinese urban youths who "ragpick" and "collect" this "garbage" upon payment of a few Chinese dollars. When the United States and Europe dumped their cut-out CDs on China, they fostered a counterculture in the fast-developing Beijing. Alienated youth, uncertain about their future in this booming market economy, are more exposed to it and part of it than ever. Official music titles are abundant on the display shelves of most CD and DVD shops, but their cost is still too high for the majority of young music fans. In fact, despite their increasing numbers, the legal CDs—mostly noncontroversial pop—were unsatisfactory to young Chinese who had grown up listening to Cui Jian and Tang Dynasty. Informal trade in saw-gash CDs "serve[d] to mitigate somewhat the ever-present tension between punk's antiauthoritarian nature and its corporate, commercial exploitation" as the illicit transactions mounted in the back-alley shacks.[3] The debris of last year's Western musical fashion had an afterlife here. Saw-gash culture "gather[ed], ironically through commodification, its subversive power, both against the dominant culture and against its state-supported forces of marketization."[4] It was a cultural phenomenon unique to China, with a generation of urban youths resisting commercialization by purchasing illegal discs with a cut. For Chinese music lovers, saw-gash is neither import nor export, but a limbo where commodities and waste blur the boundaries of the official and the banned, where their "stuff" contributes to the music industry and influences a new type of revolutionary output. The brisk *dakou* trade helped customize Chinese punk and rock and created a distinctive Beijing style and sensibility in the greater Chinese music world.

The temptation of free rock concerts and cheap chipped CDs has drawn thousands of wandering, musically aspiring kids to Beijing. Many of them are just out of school, out of their hometown, or simply out of luck. Still, these dropouts loiter in their newfound paradise. They come to the Chinese capital with their ambitions intact and their hormones ready for action. An ever-expanding and diversifying Beijing allows them to frisk and risk. Their cries are heard, their dreams shared, and their words echoed across the city by fellow bohemians. *Dakou* dealers like Lin deserve most of the credit for this phenomenon. He whets the Beijing urbanites' appetite, feeding them with genuine but illegal music, while himself achieving a relatively smooth transition from floating nobody to pirate of trade. Lin is not a mere supplier; he is also a reviewer and educator. He has a members-only website that sells his *dakou* collection, posts his music and film reviews, introduces new bands and genres, and reviews obscure films legally unavailable to Chinese audiences. The Chinese word *dakoudai,* depending on how the syllables are accented, can mean either "saw-gash tapes" or "big pockets." Inside those "big pockets" is a jumble of legal and illegal trash and treasure in both virtual and material forms. Anything and everything obscure, illegal, and discarded finds a place in these deep pockets. In recent years, as his sales of *dakou* offerings have dropped, Lin has been compensated by an exponential rise in pirated products. People like Lin both hasten and subvert an expanding Chinese market. So long as marketization is not complete, countless imperfect or substitute products—be they cut, copied, faked, diluted—fulfill a promise long undelivered under the old Communist banner of progress. The not-yet-there quality of the Chinese market is offered a taste of the promise of tomorrow in the fake and pirated product. Saw-gash offerings not only help to define the incomplete, flawed identity of the rootless urban nomads; they also forecast an exhilarating capitalist system. All those underground places and faces bring to mind a late-nineteenth-century Paris.

Like the then bohemian capital of Europe, Beijing is a meeting-place, a playground, and an incubator for disillusioned youth full of dreams. With an image as the most policed city on the ground, Beijing is also the home of the most vibrant city underground. For the novice bohemians and wannabe rockers, Beijing is a haven. It has been the capital of Chinese rock since the genre appeared in the 1980s. Widely labeled as "immoral," Beijing rockers, who were often harassed by the government if not actually arrested, came to be revered by their following as heroes. In spite of tough restrictions and mainstream opprobrium, alternative music flourishes here. The MIDI (musical instrument digital interface) modern music festival—a free rock festival organized by the Beijing MIDI School—has attracted a growing audience since its inception in 2000.[5]

49   The concrete jungle of Wudaokou.

The spiritual value of music is often most appreciated when money can't always buy the music and the music cannot be judged by its monetary value. This is how most music cultures begin and spread. It was in London that punk rock took off and dominated youth for the next few decades. In Seattle, grunge developed out of the American northwest's isolation of alternative rock scenes. In 1990s Beijing, the saw-gash generation was born of increasingly intensified globalization, with Western dumping and Chinese picking. Western garbage became the soul food for these urban kids in an age of economic optimism and opportunism. In Beijing at the height of the saw-gash years, music was played primarily to influence rather than to be consumed, an ideal that had already lost out to commercialization in the West.

Cutting into the horizon is a cluster of glass and steel skyscrapers. In the shadows below an army of wannabe anarchists drill their way into the abyss that is the suburb of Wudaokou. Yuppies in their designer suits stride on the just-paved sidewalks. Identically cropped trees line the streets. Even the shadows seem to glow with confidence and energy in the faint morning sunlight. Meanwhile the clubbers and ravers of the night before are tucked away in slumber, gathering energy for their next nocturnal activities. When they finally awake some hours later, Wudaokou will be theirs, and their vitality will transform the glimmering confidence of the nine-to-five technocrats.

Meanwhile the lives of these two groups are connected by dealers and smugglers like Lin, who supplies films and music with a passion—and a cut. He has the stuff that money can't buy: he has the knowledge that the system can't access. Either by logging in or by walking in, the saw-gash kids, rich or poor, enter the world of rejects and recycling. *Dakou* is their shared identity and memory, one that is anarchical and worldly. As the saw-gash dealers turn from smugglers into pirates, the young urbanites change from flawed-CD buyers into copyright violators. Despite the obsolescence of Beijing saw-gash culture, the lawless spirit lives on.

"Have you 'panned' today?" asks a billboard outside what looks like an ordinary office building. The billboard, however, proclaims another use for it: "Ritan Building of Commerce: The mecca for fashion panning in Beijing." Those who go in wear determined expressions on their faces and come out wearing brand names on their backs.

Inside the building are three floors of small shops. During business hours every door opens onto a haven of brand names. Some offer misspelled-name-brand dresses, others unlabeled trousers; some sell discarded but genuine designer brands. The jumble has an added value given that the building is located near the embassy district, where trees lining the boulevards conceal understated but elegant establishments.

Most of the fashion items in the Ritan Building of Commerce, as well as in other clothes-panning locations, come from a gigantic wholesaler near the Beijing Zoo. This wholesaler, allegedly the biggest in the textile sector of northern China, attracts many retailers to pan and many penurious students to "ragpick." Indeed, all those who buy at such places could be considered ragpickers as much as the denizens of Bajiacun, for many of the items for sale are essentially recycled, being rejects dumped in China by overseas manufacturers.

Fashion and garbage recur endlessly in the world of objects and desires, and nowhere is the phenomenon more manifest than the booming market of pre-Olympics Beijing. "Th[is] world . . . lives on itself," Nietzsche suggested insightfully; "its excrements are its nourishments."[6] Our waste is returned as source; as food to nourish our desires. Garbage, those traces of yesterday's trends, reinvigorates today's fashion market. Fashion, cursed at birth to die a quick death, is also blessed with a rapid return. It provides a shadow history of modern life, whereby uncanny garbage is the spectral presence that haunts. If there is a dream of modernization, then trash is the horror story. It is a horror story that modernizing Beijing does not want to know but consumes unknowingly with a missionary zeal. It is known as "fashion." It is the embodiment of modernity. Ever deceptive in its telling of time, fashion teases and seduces death, but survives itself by reviving the corpse of garbage. It knows no end, only reincarnation. When it goes out of vogue, it gets discarded and trashed in places like Bajiacun, where recyclers like Li celebrate the abundance of the preloved commodity and start the process that turns it into the fetishes of tomorrow. Like fashion, trash is eternal. Garbage of fashion, and fashion of garbage, are phenomena of modernity, the signs of progress, and the objects of entertainment. And both are doomed, rotating in the permanence that is the eternal return.

Li and Wang are not the only dreamers in Beijing. Indeed, there's no better place in China for the artist-nomads, and probably no better time to be in the capital city than the pre-Olympics present. They roam the lesser-known *hutongs* and mourn their near extinction. They may spend as little as five yuan for a street vendor's Xinjiang kebab, or ten yuan for a couple of beers. Yet they pay at least twenty yuan to "soak" (*pao*) in cafés for the better part of their day. Lounging, drinking, and deep in thought when not talking, they seem unfazed by all the hustle and bustle out there.

Yao Yao is one such person. Slightly overweight and of average height, he has a relaxed, shuffling gait that contrasts with the pace of the go-go office workers. Yao Yao is never in the suit and leather shoes that are the uniform of construction workers and city businessmen alike. Then again, he is never grumpy like the workers or discontented like many of the white-collar workers. What characterizes Yao Yao is his smell, which is an intimate blend of espresso coffee and Zhongnanhai cigarettes. Nowadays he spends most of the daytime at his café, Zakka, a few doors up from his best buddy's café, Sculpting in Time. He used to live in Sculpting until his buddy (ge'mer) suggested that they open Zakka together. Whether it was in Zakka or Sculpting it didn't matter . . . there he would be, lounging around for an afternoon over a cup of coffee and with an endless supply of cigarettes. In the café, his intense concentration on his iBook gives the impression that he is hard at work. In fact, for most of the day he is checking out the female customers and using his computer screen as a shield. When Yao Yao does have work, however, he works extremely hard. Until he started the café, Yao Yao had a series of hand-to-mouth jobs for eight years, doing odds and ends in the film industry to make ends meet. "I simply don't look for work. I wait for it to come to me," he says with an air of confidence unfound in the unemployed Chinese, some of whom are sitting on the streets outside his café. The majority of Beijing *waidiren*, or outsiders, loathe the "genetically determined" arrogance of Beijingers who live comfortably off some unreasonable state benefit or their parents' extraordinary *guanxi*. Their resentment makes Yao Yao's Taiwanese accent sound all the more pronounced. Yao Yao's confidence derives not from place, but from the idea of this place. It is the place for him to do what he has come to do.

Director Zhang Yimou was his only reason for coming to Beijing. At twenty-three, Yao Yao left his hometown of Jiayi in Taiwan for Beijing, harboring a dream of becoming the next Zhang Yimou. He had to sit a wide range of examinations before being admitted to the Beijing Film Academy (BFA), the alma mater of Zhang Yimou (*To Live*, 1994; *Hero*, 2002), Chen Kaige (winner of the Palme d'Or for *Farewell, My Concubine*, 1992), and many other notable Chinese directors. It was after Zhang and Chen gained fame that the BFA began to attract a wide range of international students as well as the very best of the local Chinese. Like most others there, Yao Yao dreamed of being a director after graduation. However, he has not made a feature film since graduating.

He came back to Beijing in 2004, after three years of working for a television station in Taiwan. "I had to return. This is where my dream began. I felt like a boy having a first-time crush—unreasonably passionate and hopeful. Nothing could stop me from falling madly for this first great love." Yao Yao's face glows as he speaks, and his eyes are fixed with a long-range gaze as though imagining his future as Zhang Yimou. Indeed, if it weren't for filmmaking, he would not have come to Beijing in the first place, and a second time, and then a third. His recurring dream is an eternal return, one that has sparked summer romance in a grand and hopeless way, but also one that has driven him into deep and dark wintry depression. Beijing is the backdrop against which his ambitions are to be tested. When Yao Yao traveled far from Beijing and his dream, he realized that he has always traveled around the center of a circle, in search of a starting point. His return is a curious one. Has he really been as free as a bird, or is he merely fluttering like a kite?

Not long ago, on a Saturday afternoon in late summer, a café across the road from the Wudaokou railway station was crowded with young people biting into sandwiches and sipping Earl Grey tea and Italian coffee. On the counter were business cards that read: "Zakka—in search of lost time." It was the opening day of Yao Yao's café. Stocked full of coffee-related products and miscellaneous items anyone could live without, the café was bustling with windowshoppers and freeloaders. Yao Yao sat with his friends on the balcony, enjoying his coffee-and-cigarette moment in the balmy weather. Around the table sat a bunch of current and former BFA students, one of them being Yao Yao's buddy Zhuangzai, co-owner of Zakka and now the sole owner of six other cafés in Beijing. We sat with them for a while and asked the obvious question, "Hey, when did you all give up on filmmaking? And why?" Zhuangzai was the first to answer. "I gave up a couple of years after graduation. I knew my limits from very early on. I just got more realistic and responsible with age, I guess." When Yao Yao answered, he did so

50   The Zakka café.

with a puff of cigarette smoke and a playful smile. "I'm in search of lost time. I just want to make films." The cigarette smoke reflects on his spectacles, hanging around like the customers after free coffee, then drifts off as they do, finally vanishing into thin air.

Meet Jane Huang. She runs a restaurant called Private Kitchen. Taking a traditional Beijing courtyard house and converting it into an elegant, discreet restaurant in this part of town was a risky business, but Jane is a woman who likes to take chances. You cannot miss or mistake her as you enter the courtyard of her private kitchen . . . And it is, in a very obvious way, her private kitchen. Tucked away from the tourists in the backstreets of Xiguan Lane, Jiaodaokou, this world bears traces of Jane, past and imagined.

She has, for many Chinese, lived the promise of one world, one dream (the slogan of the coming Beijing Olympic Games). After graduating from a fine Beijing university, she studied overseas before returning to China and launching Private Kitchen. Each part of Jane's life is reflected somewhere on the restaurant walls and in its furnishings. Her mother was the vice-chancellor of a prominent university, and Jane's gentle, even-toned, unaccented Mandarin distinguishes her speech from the sharp and sometimes raucous tones of the neighborhood's *hutongs*. Her English has a tiny Australian lilt. Jane is part of another eternal return, the returned student.

As we are ushered into one of five dining rooms, Jane explains that the restaurant hasn't officially opened yet, and a few parts still need some final touches. This room is adorned with several framed photographs of Tasmania. Escorting us to a square wooden table, Jane sets before us some rare Guizhou-style dishes combined with just a touch of European elegance.

It would make a great surrealist headline: "Sichuanese woman studies business in Australia, goes to Beijing, and opens a Guizhou Restaurant!" "Cooking was only my hobby," explains Jane. "I never intended to make a career out of it." In fact, Jane's main reason for opening up the restaurant was that it enabled her to stay in Beijing. "I love Beijing. This is my favorite city," she says. She knows about cities. She has lived not only in cities abroad but also in most of the major Chinese cities, including Chengdu, Guangzhou, Shanghai, and, again and again, Beijing.

We listen while eating one of her specialties: sour fish soup. This version is trout cooked in a slowly stewed ginger, tomato, and pineapple base and topped with a little chili and basil. It's hard to find such southwestern minority dishes in Beijing, much less in this part of town.

Yet there is no notion of the authentic in Jane's rendition of southwestern cuisine. Pleased by our compliments, she takes a puff on her cigarette and tells us that one group of customers was so displeased with the change of taste from traditional Guizhou fare that they didn't want to pay. In cooking, Chinese dislike the hybrid. This attitude is perhaps best captured in the negative connotations attached to the word *bianwei*, which means a change in taste. In Beijing, when it comes to food, most chase after the restaurants with cuisines that promise *zhengzong*, meaning the authentic or genuine. Few will venture from this path, but those who do may also venture off the path in other ways. That potential is what makes Beijing a vibrant, bohemian city.

At the end of the meal, Jane makes a graceful but final exit. Her service is untypical of Beijing, where waitresses usually leave abruptly and without any concern for the customer. A few minutes later, as we leave the courtyard, we see her with a group of workers, but she moves off, evading our attempts to bid farewell. We pass through the gate and back into another Beijing, the Beijing of the Xiguan area committee, with its very different dream, yet a shared world.

This young, art-aspiring bunch of whom Yao Yao and Jane are examples is humorously called *beipiao*, or northern drifters. They come from all parts of China. They are here to try their luck and follow their fate in the *jianghu* tradition of Beijing. The Chinese word *jianghu* literally means streams and lakes. Often used in the context of martial arts, *jianghu* is the space, the universe, for wandering heroes and assassins alike. In modern Beijing, these knights-errant have been replaced by wandering artists, writers, directors, and other bohemian types. Nevertheless, bonding and loyalty remain the ticket to any specific group membership. Forming their own circles according to skill and aspiration or sect and discipline, the northern drifters can be said to *hun* together—or mix with others and do odds and ends—in the murky waters of Beijing *jianghu*.

Whether we attribute it to the pulling power of symbols, an economic boom, or the special power of *qi* still wafting through the capital, Beijing draws to itself the alternative, the marginal, the rebellious, and the underappreciated. While government bureaucrats draw a map of the city that clearly marks out their runaway success, these "northern drifters" muddy the waters with a more opaque form of development. They are what give this city its edge, its interest, and its quirky little corners.

Beijing returned as the political and cultural center of China after it was reestablished as the capital in 1949. It took political power from Nanjing and cultural power from Shanghai. While Republican-era Nanjing faded, Shanghai, once proclaimed "the Paris of the East," also lost its luster. This port city that had long ago opened itself to a vast number of foreign goods and people had once been regarded as the "key to modern China," but its image was fixed as bourgeois, feminine, and sentimental.[7] Beijing quickly broke with its traditional, dynastic image, asserting its renewed importance with the relocation from Nanjing of several prestigious academic and cultural institutes. Since 1978 it has been the epicenter of numerous philosophical, cultural, musical, and artistic movements, boasting four generations of artists, five generations of filmmakers, and China's founding rock musicians. Names such as Zhang Yimou, Chen Kaige, and Cui Jian are among the better known, but there are many more. Most of these artists/musicians came from all over China, but it was in Beijing that they made their names. Whereas Shanghai had eagerly "Westernized" itself and developed a hybrid image as an orientalized sophisticated city, Beijing continued to absorb, internalize, and display a vast array of Chinese culture. The rapid expansion of the city, however aesthetically distasteful it might look from the outside, reflects an ever more tolerant *qi* that has drawn in all the crouching tigers and hidden dragons of the surrounding countryside. On the ground, Beijing *jianghu* harbors many hidden charms. The immediate charm of commerce-oriented Shanghai once attracted foreigners as the "key to modern China," but Beijing, with its swirling winds and clouds of dust, has become the new gateway to the modern.

Hong Kong writer Chen Guangzhong appreciatively described Beijing as the bohemian capital of China. He opts for the term "bohemian" over the buzzword "New Beijing School" because contemporary Beijing culture encompasses much more than the term "school" suggests. The New Beijing School as labeled by cultural commentators is confined to contemporary Beijing literature and academic thought written mostly by those who graduated from Peking and Tsinghua universities. These writers style their work in rather lofty moralistic terms or in folksy parochial ones. Yet the vibrancy of this city is better captured by the alternative writers and artists, who enjoy massive popularity and influence at the margins.

The "bohemian trend" began in 1985 with Beijing writer Liu Suola's *You Got No Other Choice (Ni bie wu xuanze)* and Xu Xing's *Untitled Transposition (Wu zhuti biandiao).*[8] The two works heralded the arrival of a Chinese "beat generation." Wang Shuo, another Beijing author who became a national cultural icon, invented what was later called the "hooligan style of writing" *(pizi wenxue),* in which the Chinese Communist Party cadres and their children are satirized for their arrogance and lack of cool. The undercurrents of this new ethos slowly formed a bohemian wave that has revitalized the Beijing qi.

This trend took off in earnest in the 1990s, when the economic boom of reform began to refashion the city. Chinese youth, lured by the budding "cool" of Beijing, formed an alternative bohemian capital. The new era was heralded by Cui Jian's national tour, evocatively and appropriately called "The New Long March." It all started in the Beijing Workers' Stadium, where Cui played his hits such as "Nothing to My Name" and "Starting from Scratch," which resonated with the young northern Chinese. His music and his commitment to Chinese rock and roll fired the imagination of thousands of young people and inspired them to move to Beijing and pursue their dreams. Today it is Beijing—not the commercial hub Shanghai or the industrial center Guangzhou—that dominates China's rock scene. The congregation of young, wannabe rockers contrasts with the myriad army units in this city of paradoxes.

It's Jane back at the Private Kitchen who tells us about this. "This is the place where there are the most police and army forces in the whole of China, yet if you stay in Beijing as a businessperson who is not interested in challenging the authority of the Communist Party, you have just as much freedom as people in the West, if not more." She takes another puff of her cigarette before continuing: "Once you're established and have built up a bit of a *guanxi* network, there are always backdoors to get through in order to solve problems." Everybody has backdoors in this place, and the net effect is that virtually anything is possible. It is a world that contains just the right explosive contradictions that incite and nurture artistic creation.

Like nineteenth-century Paris, Beijing today is transforming its bohemian art into a marketable commodity. Works by the poor artists of the former Yuanmingyuan village and today's Tongzhou, twelve miles from central Beijing, are widely exhibited overseas.

Just as with the New British Cool of the 1990s, it is the artists out-side the art school system who have suddenly caught the attention of international dealers. The sheer luck enjoyed by a small number of Beijing-based artists encouraged many other aspiring artists and enterprising (con) artists to become involved in the Chinese avant-garde movement. Titillated by chance, an army of people came to try their luck here, and before long the capital that had once been a political hub became an epicenter of a bohemian art world.

"By 'bohemians,' I mean that class of individuals for whom existence is a problem, circumstances a myth, and fortune an enigma; who have no sort of fixed abode, no place of refuge; who belong nowhere and are met with everywhere; who have no par-ticular calling in life but follow fifty professions; who are ready to live honestly if they can, and otherwise if they cannot," wrote Adolphe d'Ennery and Grangé about the Parisian bohemians of 1843.[9] They were vagrants in Paris when that scene started. From 1800 on, unknown and self-proclaimed artists moved into the cheaper parts of Paris and mingled with the Gypsies and vagabonds. Beijing's bohemians are today's counterparts to that Parisian trend. The city is the perfect playground for those who want to experiment and to create something new. Trash in Bajia-cun discloses passé trends that are destined to creep back onto dis-play shelves, while fashion ends up as trash when it appears at the wrong place and wrong time. For drifters in Beijing today, however, there's no better place or time to be. As a Beijing friend once said, "This is an era of Pangu universal opening." Pangu is a mythic char-acter who created the world by separating the earth and the sky. Modern Beijing is like this embryonic form, a gray and chaotic world that still offers the promise of life and great possibilities. Romantics see the earth upheaved, and when you wander off the official map, you will see it too.

5 AUTHENTICITY

On a freezing Friday night, Mr. Yang is out cruising in his five-year-old Hyundai with his new "friends." In actuality, they are not friends at all, but business partners, and Mr. Yang is out to impress. After a ten-course feast that we could never hope to finish, Mr. Yang spirits us all off for a spot of karaoke—commonly known as KTV in China. The karaoke bar we go to is a nationwide franchise called Cashbox Partyworld (Qiangui), and it's an import from Taiwan. It even has "loyalty cards" for frequent customers.

Mr. Yang has collected plenty of points because he comes to this bar often, even though he is no great fan of karaoke. Neither are his "friends." They are all simply playing their part in the elaborate game that in China is called *la guanxi* (to connect). "You need to build up strong *guanxi* to get ahead in this place," Yang explains. "To get anything done around here you have to be able to pull strings," he says out of earshot of his companions. "Oh, and one other thing: around here, please don't call me Mr. Yang. It's too formal. Call me Yang *dage!*" . . . All of a sudden Mr. Yang, whom we have known for only a brief time, has become our "big brother," or *dage*. He knows, as do we, that he is no more a big brother to us than we are siblings to him. Nevertheless, in performing as though he is our big brother, while keeping the public secret that he is not, we have taken our first steps toward cementing our *guanxi* relations with him. As the night unfolds, our *guanxi* develops over chilled beers, heavy smoking, and some crazy off-key singing.

The tunes they sing are a mixture of love songs and revolutionary anthems of yesteryear. In both cases they are about emotional connectedness. So, too, is this notion of *guanxi*. We recall its workings in the Maoist gift economy that once politicized everything in Chinese life. But when that revolutionary era died away, *guanxi* did not. Instead it reappeared in a slightly different form to reaffirm the affective familial relations that appeared so central to life in the backstreets of Jiaodaokou. Now, in a karaoke bar, late on a drunken Friday night, it makes yet another appearance. Same word, same familial references, same degree of tactility, but this time it is being pressed into the service of a very different set of ends. So what, then, do we take from this as authentic *guanxi?*

Led into a dimly lit room by an attractive young woman, our companions immediately go into song-selection mode and punch in codes to bring up the music for their upcoming performances. Within ten minutes a pall of smoke hangs over the darkened room; within twenty minutes they have all become boisterous, and within half an hour we are just one more roomful of drunken, glazed-eyed businessmen letting off steam by telling Frankie boy Sinatra that we did it our way.

Jugs of chilled beer appear, cartons of cigarettes are consumed, and someone's favorite song pops up on the menu (song list). This may not be the stuff of great social change, but it has certainly managed to change the faces of this crowd. It's hard to imagine that these wannabe crooners are, by day, devoted Party men, and it's even harder to understand how it is that they know all the latest hits from Hong Kong and Taiwan, and can even sing them fluently in Cantonese! There is obviously a lot of KTV under their belts. In between Mandarin and Cantonese songs, some in our group even choose a couple of English golden oldies. The buttoned-up business suits of Beijing turn into party animals when the KTV spotlight falls on them.

The microphone numbs our aural capacity while the darkness stimulates fantasies of stardom. As the night wears on with more cheap booze, noise becomes symphony, strangers become brothers, and ordinary people become megastars. Memory resurrects old dreams and sentiments via the magic mike of the karaoke bar.

Much of the fun of karaoke rests upon role-playing and self-discovery through the individual's song choice. *Karaoke* is a Japanese coinage meaning "empty orchestra" (combining *kara,* "empty," with *oke,* the short form of an English loanword, "orchestra"), and it is the job of the crooner to fill the empty void and thus achieve temporary stardom. Paradoxically, these acts of impersonation bring out an authentic (part of) self that is otherwise hidden from view. And it takes the public secret of *guanxi* relations to help reveal it. For Brother Yang, the key to establishing these strong *guanxi* connections is to touch upon and share the emotional side of life, and thereby forge a bond with people he has to work with.

It often takes some coaxing to get a virgin karaoke performer up onstage, but once someone's there, performance proves addictive. The experience of displaying one's vocal ability to prerecorded orchestral accompaniment is less threatening to the notion of self than people might imagine; besides, the comprehensive lyric cues on the videos help the crooners achieve a safe performance. Some advanced karaoke systems, we're told, can even adjust the key of the musical accompaniment to the singers and can grade their performance according to the degree of resemblance to the prerecorded tunes and the lyric cue balls. At the end of each performance, the accompanying video will cue spectators to applaud or, failing that, provide canned applause of its own. Here is the road to stardom without the risk of failure.

Sounds of yelling, clapping, clinking, not to mention the blaring and echoing voices amplified through stereo speakers, make the five-hour sing-along an oddly harmonious affair. What holds the discordant notes of the "empty orchestra" together is not the corrections offered by the karaoke machine, but the principle of social harmony that Chinese call "face." As Yang plays the role of an exuberant but cautious conductor, his exhilarated though musically challenged ensemble plays along to his tune. He guides us through the night with competence and subtlety. Within ten minutes of our arrival at Cashbox Partyworld, he has coaxed everyone into contributing to the song play list, filling it up with twenty-odd numbers. In less than an hour, everyone has had a fair share of singing without any reports of stage fright. From the second hour on, he ensures that any initial timidity has evaporated and, between the microphones and beer bottles, the "empty orchestra" goes on performing in perfect harmony with the feeling of the evening.

According to The Encyclopedia of Japanese Pop Culture, "making a visit to a karaoke bar [is] a test of endurance until you get your own turn at the mike (and a chance to take revenge on your tormentors)."[1] But our Friday night seems more like an exercise in giving and receiving face. Giving face is a key part of karaoke etiquette. One sits and observes, takes one's turn at the mike, claps after each performance, and offers an endless string of compliments to the performer. The popular belief that karaoke makes a public display of self-expression is only half true. So is the idea that karaoke singing is about celebrity impersonation.

Consider the following: to boost the singer's confidence, the group gives verbal encouragement before the performance, applauds or encourages between verses, and claps at the end, while discreetly and politely ignoring every shortcoming.[2] Assuring a positive response involves considerable work, but the result is always a bit of an ego boost for the performer. These highly predictable and staged performances are made even safer by song-related video images and the dancing cue balls. During the performances no one can engage in meaningful conversation; instead everyone busily browses through the song list in anticipation of his or her own performance or, under the influence of alcohol, uncritically cheers someone on. The postmodern cliché of "disorderly order" aptly describes the karaoke atmosphere.

Equally fascinating is the performance itself. While singing along to the videos and dancing cue balls, third-rate on-screen models look blankly into the distance. The video clips may be unoriginal, but they can still tap into emotions. Inside a soundproof and darkened room, we leave behind the dog-eat-dog worlds of politics and business and enter the mushy and sentimental universe of the love song. Just as there are thousands of songs to pick from, so, too, are there numerous personas to try to emulate. One of Brother Yang's clients, Xiaolong, who arrived as a quiet and cold-faced young man, transforms himself into a star, offering a virtuoso performance of nearly twenty songs in four different languages. The rest of us then take our turns in a mimetic exercise that, in the words of Walter Benjamin and René Girard, "allows people to connect to other people, and also invites one to locate one's own alterity."[3]

In these performances, recreation becomes re-creation. Through star emulation, ordinary individuals get an opportunity to imagine and achieve self-reinvention. A karaoke performance attempts a very personal negotiation between the private and public spheres, between fantasy and reality, between sentiment and etiquette. At nearly three in the morning, Brother Yang and his clients wrap up their evening business. After a night filled with masquerades and confessions and between cues and impromptu performances, they have bonded. The alcohol in them gradually dissipates, and, under the spotlight, only empty bottles and cigarette butts are left on the table. The real residue of the karaoke session is *guanxi*, which will live on well beyond this night.

Karaoke is not the only site where public performance and social bonding are enacted. Indeed, one might even think of this as a trait of "old Beijing."

"Here you come. This way!" yell a couple of boys as we walk into the restaurant with Brother Yang and his family. Those eating inside remain focused on what is on their plates and take no notice of the noise surrounding our entrance. They sit at old-fashioned wooden tables on old-fashioned wooden stools, roaring with laughter while noisily munching away. In contrast to most restaurants around the city, in this old-style Beijing tavern there are no waitresses, only waiting boys. Nor are the boys called *fuwuyuan,* or waiters. Here, in the Haiwanju restaurant, they are called *dian-xiao'er,* or "little seconds." Wearing a traditional round black satin cap, a white top with a white hand towel draped over one arm, black satin trousers that match the cap, white socks, and black cotton shoes, these youngsters quickly lead us to our table, yelling and joking among themselves, not even bothering to offer us a fake smile. While we order our food, they don't waste time looking us in the eye; they're far busier with their own cheeky boyish humor, which is as infectious as it can be insulting. They make fun of our ignorance as they pour our tea. Beijing, these days, swallows as much of this style as it can get. The "little seconds" yell out our orders in a thick Beijing drawl that is unintelligible to most customers.

Always crowded, the Haiwanju restaurant is a scene from old Beijing. It captures and amplifies what every Beijing restaurant already has, and that is *renao*. Literally meaning "hot and noisy," *renao* is a style unknown in up-market restaurants in the West, where the restrained and elegant are the order of the day. And in Beijing, no place is more *renao* than Haiwanju.

With a front as wide as Kmart and lighting as bright as McDonald's, this cavernous restaurant in Ganjiakou, in the Haidian District, claims to offer "old Beijing" style with "authentic" Beijing food. Brother Yang tells us he likes to bring his family here because the food is so delicious and so authentically Beijing. "This is unbeatably the best-value restaurant in Beijing—scrumptious food served in enormous portions for very little money!" The name of the restaurant says it all. *Haiwan* means "an ocean in a bowl," and *ju* means "residence" or "place." In old Beijing slang, then, it could be translated as "the residence of ocean bowls" or, perhaps more intelligibly, the place where one gets a really large bowl. Given the size of the bowls and the satisfied faces, the place is well named, and the *renao* that imbues the little seconds' performance is infectious.

The Yang family are clearly enjoying themselves, grabbing the menu and insisting that they are paying for us, their guests. What they are in fact doing is paying homage to yet another old Beijing custom. This is not the land of going Dutch, and as Mr. Yang orders

51   Hot and noisy Haiwanju.

an endless string of Beijing delicacies the costumed boys pour our tea and yell, joke, and explain each dish. The dishes come quickly with names that seem strange and tastes that are obviously acquired: *baodu,* or "popped stomach," is sliced sheep's stomach; *chaogan,* or "fried liver," is a starchy soup made up of pork intestines, liver, and garlic paste; *madoufu* isn't *doufu* (tofu, soybean curd) at all, but a green-bean paste, tasting strongly of yeast and looking like a brown mudslide nearly covering a pile of spring onions and chilis. If the looks don't repel, the smells just might. *Douji,* unfiltered soybean milk, has such a pungent odor that when it lands on our table even the people next to us hold their noses.

Not everything is quite as exotic and strange to the tastebuds as these dishes, even if the names of them are. The names of imperial court desserts, such as *ludagun,* or "rolling donkeys," and *tang'erduo,* or "sugared ears," reflect a visual association rather than a summary of ingredients. While such specialty dishes feature in many Beijing restaurants (including this one), Haiwanju is renowned for a very simple concoction called *zhajiangmian.* Part of what makes this dish famous is the performance of the little seconds as they assemble it. Here they come, carrying to our table an ocean-sized bowl of noodles, a myriad of smaller bowls holding vegetables, and a still smaller bowl filled with meat sauce. Within seconds they have tipped each of our bowls into the noodles, added the other ingredients, and placed the *zhajiangmian* before us with a dash of panache.

For Beijingers like Brother Yang and his family, there is always a sense of romance about this authentic Beijing food served in a genuine Beijing way. The accent, the uniform, the service, and, most significantly, the dishes are reminiscent of an older time in Beijing. Likewise the freewheeling and *renao* style of this street-level example of "old Beijing" is very different from the stiff formality of the imperial-era lifestyle captured gastronomically in *gongtingcai,* or imperial court food. Qing court food, such as the famous Peking roast duck or the Mongolian hot pot, will never grace the table of a restaurant like Haiwanju, which, in a form of inverted snobbery, prides itself in offering the authentic local street food of old Beijing.

Brother Yang holds forth on its virtues. He tells us that this place opened in late 2001, after the owners had researched "old Beijing" recipes and recovered them. "Authentic" street-level Beijing food, such as *yangshuangchang* (frosted lamb sausages) and *huokua dunhuangyu* (fish stewed over a very low flame), he asserts confidently, was saved from extinction by this very restaurant.

As Brother Yang waxes lyrical about the virtues of this place as the savior of part of "old Beijing," we wonder how people actually conduct research on street delicacies. Yang has culled most of his information from a blurb in a guidebook. But these specialties are, by definition, of the street and not of "the book." Without cookbooks or detailed records, the food being presented is as much guesswork as it is recovery. Moreover, this "traditional" popular Beijing street food that Brother Yang now values so much was never part of the Beijing in which he grew up. The traditional dishes from his youth are very different. Growing up in the Cultural Revolution, Brother Yang ate buns and millet porridge. His family was luckier than most others because his mother was a much-revered heroine of the Korean War. As a result, his family was allocated meat once a fortnight. Meat he might have had, but the condiments, seasonings, and exotic ingredients needed to make Haiwanju's "street food" would have been unobtainable in those days. Nor is this food part of the world of his children. It is no longer commonly eaten in the homes of ordinary Beijingers or even on the street. Indeed, the "popular," "traditional," "authentic" "old Beijing" food being served in Haiwanju is as exotic to Yang and his family as it is to us. This is, in fact, Beijing food in fancy dress, a Beijing tradition as a theme park, an "old Beijing" that is as much performance as recovery.

More than through anything else, it is through food that we discover a very Chinese trait. There is a persisting desire here to recover the authentic that perhaps no longer resonates in quite the same way in the West. Indeed, the word *zhengzong*, which means authentic or genuine, is possibly the most ubiquitous and powerful gastronomic signifier to be found around the city. Prominently displayed on the front window of every second restaurant, the two characters that produce *zhengzong* flag a significant cultural difference under the sign of gastronomy. Cosmopolitan Beijing has not joined the trend toward hybrid cuisine seen in Western capitals. Instead, this is a city that craves authenticity.

There are signs of this desire for the old and authentic everywhere. Old-fashioned teahouses started to spring up in the area around Qianmen in the 1980s. "Old Beijing" recipes, customs, and pastimes have come back into vogue as the authenticity industry has taken off in the post-economic-reform era, and numerous Qing-era courtyard houses have been saved from demolition and restored as the property boom put a premium on such spaces. *Hutong* tours by rickshaw drivers, launched as late as 2000, have helped preserve many old shops close to bankruptcy and led to the development of new businesses in the historical conservation areas. In many ways, Beijing has been rediscovering its prerevolutionary self through increasingly intensified commercialization. Authenticity is a red-hot trade in a reinvented Beijing.

"Walk slowly, customers!" yell the boys. Satiated with a feast à la authentic Beijing, we waddle with the Yang family down the narrow passageway out of Haiwanju. Making our way past talking birds that squawk out "good-bye," we reach the exit, where the little seconds also squawk good-bye to us and greet a new batch of customers. *Renao* has become a way of life here, and the little seconds send us off in the same flippant way they invited us in. Their shrill voices combine with those of the squawking birds and the boisterous crowd inside the restaurant, blurring into one loud cacophonous chant: welcome to old Beijing!

There is an urban myth here that the "real" Beijing can be found only in the *hutongs* and possibly in the Communist-era work units. In the old alleyways, people's faces are weathered by the passings of seasons, dynasties, and regimes; their clothing styles seem frozen in a period somewhere between Maoism and economic reform; and their accents are laden with the guttural r that makes the Beijing "dialect" so unintelligible to anyone living outside the *hutongs*. Compared with the people living in high-rise apartments, *hutong* residents appear to enjoy a leisurely life outside the mad rush of development. Theirs is a world with time on its hands. They roam the alleyways and streets, walking their little Pekingese dogs or carrying beautifully carved bamboo cages with budgies, parrots, or other singing birds inside. Their world is one of display. Showing the talents of their birds, the beauty of their cages, or the cuteness of their dogs to neighbors and friends seems to be the main point of this public performance. If so, it's a facet of life that has been around for a while. Publicly feeding one's caged bird is said to have been a pastime in the imperial era. It was still a pastime of the rich and famous until the Chinese Communist Party took over and branded it as unforgivably decadent. Now the practice has revived, but among ordinary people. Now large numbers of city residents receiving unknown government benefits are luxuriating in what appears to be a permanent holiday.

Around midday, after a morning's stroll, these people of the *hutongs* often drop in at a friend's place in the confident expectation that lunch will be provided. This drop-in culture is widespread in Beijing. It is yet another small part of the gift economy. After lunch they may stick around and spend the afternoon with their friends, drinking tea and eating pumpkin seeds while gossiping about the goings-on in the neighborhood. On afternoons in late summer we see these people sitting outside their overcrowded courtyard compounds on little bamboo stools, fanning the breeze, smoking, chatting, playing Chinese chess or poker. If they are playing a game, they often get gratuitous advice from the ubiquitous crowd that seems equally intent on whiling away the hours and shooting the breeze. Their shared sense of time seems to have frozen once their working lives have come to an end. They live to kill time, undisturbed by the dust swirling through a myriad of construction sites or by the blaring noise of the city traffic that is choking all the streets around their tiny enclaves.

This part of Beijing is full of *ye* (a Chinese equivalent of esquires), who can afford to live in this leisurely way. Though proud that their city has been chosen as an events venue, these Beijingers aren't all that rapt about the consequences. For them, the Olympics craze detracts from the tranquillity and languid pace of their daily life. They also look down on *waidiren*, or outsiders (excluding foreigners), who are commonly thought to lack culture and act like pragmatists. *Waidiren*, for their part, claim that the Beijingers walk and talk as though they were lords of the city. Beijingers, they add, have this sense of pride because emperors and Mao once made this place their home. Beijingers are proud of the Forbidden City, of the developments around the coming Olympics, of Peking duck, and even of pizzas. They will readily agree with the cliché that "the twenty-first century belongs to China and China belongs to Beijing" and will wax lyrical about the capital's cultural jewels. But if we criticize certain specific things about the city, they will join in with alacrity. It is said that Beijingers share these traits with New Yorkers, but, in so many ways, Beijing really is a world of its own.

To those who are not natives of this city, Beijingers may appear an arrogant, lazy bunch. It is claimed that they manage to avoid work by living off the generous government subsidies they have received since the time of Mao Zedong, and that because they have resided in this ancient place longer than anyone else, they feel they

52   Languid Beijingers.

should be treated with special regard. They are said to have a million impossible ambitions in their heads, but they are also said to be all mouth.[4] They think they are better than outsiders because they live in the Chinese capital, which is home to the majority of the country's bureaucrats as well as many of the rich and famous. Because they are often well connected, jobs just seem to fall in their way. They need only to pick and choose, so they become very picky. They complain about the flood of migrant workers in their city, about their lowbrow ways and their pragmatism, ignoring the fact that today's Beijing is largely sustained by an army of poorly treated outsiders who do the jobs that Beijingers themselves will not touch. According to a newspaper survey of the residents of four Chinese cities—Beijing, Shanghai, Chongqing, and Hong Kong—Beijingers are the most romantic while Hong Kong denizens are the most pragmatic.[5] In his praise of this aspect of Beijing, Hong Kong commentator Chen Guanzhong writes rapturously:

> Beijing really is charismatic. At every art event, you get to see a number of grotesque male figures who never wash their hair but are always in the company of beautiful women. So long as those slobs have a market, it proves the undying romanticism of Beijing. Of course, this is not entirely true. Today's Beijing has caught up with the rest of the country in that money, not romanticism, is now the ultimate way to attract women. But if you don't have money, it's really not the end of the world. You'd score very well as a westerner. But if you aren't a westerner, you can try to be an artist.[6]

Beijingers are flaky, and so are those attracted to this city. They daydream, convinced that the world is theirs for the taking.

Not only the outsiders, but also the Beijingers themselves perpetuate these sorts of stereotypes about the city's inhabitants. The abundance of antiques and imperial architecture easily deludes visitors into believing that there is a historic presence haunting all Beijingers. Yet the accents of ten random pedestrians in the city center leave the impression that this is really a city of migrants. Every second person appears to have an accent deriving from somewhere else. Even in the "conservation zone" *hutongs,* accents and dialects of all sorts—Chinese and foreign—can be heard. "Old Beijingers"—those whose families have lived in the city for three generations or more—are pretty hard to find. Having been the backdrop to various twentieth-century revolutions, mass movements, and political campaigns, Beijing has been shaken up so many times that there are few true Old Beijingers left.

Even Brother Yang, who has lived in the city for forty years, says he isn't really an authentic Beijinger. His family moved here from Yunan when he was nine, after his mother had fought in the Korean War. When he travels, he tells people he's from Beijing, but when asked for his "hometown" he still names Yunan. Now that he is growing older, his dream is to return to the warm climate of that province.

"Beijing is so dry, so crowded, so noisy, and so expensive," he grumbles. He wonders why anyone would want to live here and marvels at the huge waves of migration into the city. In fact, he knows only too well why people come. Money, power, and fame are the great forces driving this latest wave of immigrants. In some ways, today's new Beijingers are not all that different from migrants to other cosmopolitan centers like London or New York— bourgeois and bohemian, romantic and pragmatic, poetic and scientific, perfumed and odoriferous. They live the Olympic motto of "One World, One Dream." The difference lies in the scope of the cosmopolitanism: whereas London and New York draw peoples from every land, Beijing draws peoples from every part of China. It is therefore less one world, one dream than one China, one dream. From London to Beijing, however, the dream remains the same.

In 1993 Chinese avant-garde director Zhang Yuan made a film about Beijing's street kids that could well have been a Chinese version of the 1996 British cult classic *Trainspotting*. Zhang's *Beijing Bastards* engages with the lives of the members of an unknown punk rock band that cannot find a venue, and includes characters such as a helpless, pregnant girlfriend of one band member, an underground musician desperate to sell his songs, and a destitute artist who is fixated on painting only one human. Such "Beijing drifters," as those ambitious but vagrant city nomads are now called, give the capital an edgy, artistic feel. The imminent arrival of the 2008 Olympics has accelerated this sense of artistic edginess to produce a distinctive internationalization.

On the streets, cab drivers try out their patchy English while foreigners try out their broken Chinese. "Old Beijingers" are only a tiny part of this new metropolis that celebrates its own diversity and hybridity. Zhang Yuan's *Beijing Bastards* was able to capture something of this city largely because Beijing is, in fact, a bastard city. Lacking the decadence of Shanghai's fin-de-siècle splendor, Beijing's Chinese cosmopolitanism derives uniquely from a bohemian invasion of modern China's dreamers and losers. It is cosmopolitanism with Chinese characteristics, but it also exposes the myth of the "Beijinger." Beijing is more of an idea or ethos than a place of origin. Beijing connotes vastness, power, fantasy, desire, eccentricity, hybridity, chance, luck, tension, and a certain explosiveness. Indeed, when Chinese rock pioneer Cui Jian exploded onto center stage twenty years ago, he pretty much got this city right. Standing on the stage before an audience in Beijing's Workers' Stadium, he screamed out to the crowd: "The first moment you arrive in Beijing, you're already a Beijinger. Yes, Beijingers are bastards."[7] How prescient Cui Jian's provocation turned out to be.

In Beijing, as throughout China, birth certificates, identification cards, household registration, graduation certificates, receipts,

53   Sorting-out registration.

work permits, business licenses, and drivers' licenses are all a necessity. Those who lack such documents keep a very low profile. For outsiders, "sorting-out registration" is now the ticket to most jobs in the city.

Some version of the two characters for the word *banzheng,* "arrange registration or certification," and a phone number beneath them greet every Beijinger on the way to and from work. But advertisements for "sorting-out registration" are an altogether different matter, reflecting guerrilla tactics. They are advertisements for forgers spray-painted onto half-knocked-down walls and pavements near construction sites and slums. They vie with the character *chai*—meaning "to demolish"—for dominance of these city streets. Some appear in wealthier areas, but most are found in the streets teeming with migrants. What graffiti are to London, this type of ad is to Beijing.

Today, outsiders' access to a job in Beijing is now only a secret fee and a phone call away. Forgery has become something of a standard service in this city; some specialist forgers are able to recreate special-purpose documents such as professional pregnancy-test results, hygiene certificates, marriage papers, and, of course, divorce papers. To dial the number and engage the services of a forger is one way to *banshi,* or "take care of business." And *banzheng* is the easiest avenue to *banshi.*

Some of the ads appear without text, yet everyone knows what they offer. The eleven-digit numbers of cell phones sprayed on city pavements and walls provide a magic code that may help a newcomer break into the job market. This city applauds performance, and the more one appears to perform, the more likely one is to be successful. Thus the presence of these ads reflects the tempo of this city and its moods, its legal laxities, and the privileges it accords. For strangers who have arrived in Beijing without the means to survive, "sorting-out registration" offers a passport to success. As one of the spray-painted slogans on the street promises, "There are only those things you can't think of. There's nothing we can't do."[8]

Brother Yang told me about a young girl from Gansu whom he knew who rang one of these numbers. Lili came to Beijing after graduating from high school. She had to leave her hometown because in 2001, just before her final year of high school, her father, a high-ranking official in the provincial government, had been sentenced to seventeen years' imprisonment on corruption charges. As a result of her father's disgrace, her mother also lost her job as a secretary on the county council. As Lili's life crumbled, her grades dropped through the floor, and with the family's financial situation steadily worsening, Lili decided that as soon as she finished high school, in the summer of 2002, she would come to Beijing with a former classmate from primary school named Sumei, who had lived in the city for two years and was about to return there after a visit home.

The train ride from Gansu took a little over a day. When the two girls arrived in Beijing, Sumei lent Lili 200 yuan (26 U.S. dollars) to help tide her over until she found a job. In this city, jobs require certification, and Sumei pointed out how to get them as they walked past the "sorting-out registration" ads along the street. "You're a smart girl," she said. "You always got good grades, and on top of that, you look well educated. If you tell a job recruiter that you did a two-year vocational course at such-and-such a school, they'll believe you. With a fake certificate you'll land a well-paid secretarial job. You should try one of those numbers."

Lili took the plunge and dialed a number.

After a few rings, a woman with a southern accent answered.

"What kind of certificates do you do?" Lili asked apprehensively.

"Anything. You name it, we do it. What do you want?"

"I want to get a diploma from a vocational school."

"No problem. Just tell me what school you want and what year you want us to say you graduated. You also need to give us your personal details."

"How much will it cost?" asked Lili.

"Three hundred [yuan] for just the certificate, 600 if it comes with the file, and 1,200 if you want us to put it up on the web."

"On the web?" Lili repeated the last three words with a tinge of disbelief.

"So that they can search out the school certificate on the web like it's the genuine article."

"Where are you? How do I find you?"

"How can I tell you where I am? If you want it, just give me a call."

"Are you really in Beijing? How come your number shows you're outside Beijing?"

"We'd be found out if it was a Beijing number. A non-Beijing number gives us more anonymity. Hey, you better decide now. I'm knocking off work soon," said the woman impatiently.

"All right. I'll get just the certificate. Can we make the deal? Is 250 yuan okay with you? You know, I'm from a poor family, and I've just arrived in Beijing. I'm short of money and desperate to get a job at the minute."

"Well . . . we don't normally give discounts. But we'll make it 270 just this once. Two hundred seventy yuan is my last offer. Do you want it or not?"

"Okay, I'll do it for 270. What should I call you?"

"You can call me Ms. Zhang."

Lili borrowed another 100 yuan from Sumei, a move that pushed their friendship to the brink, but she had no choice. She then telephoned Ms. Zhang to get instructions about how to deposit the payment. First she was given details about the bank account. Then she was told that a van would be parked just outside the bank at the appointed meeting time. While Lili went in to deposit the money, the people in the van would forge the certificate. When she had deposited the money, she would phone them so that they could check that the transaction had gone through. If everything was fine, they would then give her the certificate.

Lili made her way anxiously to the bank, fearing that she might not get the fake certificate or, worse, that she might lose her friendship with Sumei as well as the money. In the worst-case scenario, she would get caught by the police and lose everything. At eighteen, she had never had to go to a bank before, and she certainly had never done anything illegal like this before. When she thought about this, her heart skipped a beat. Suddenly she had an image of her father: he must have done such shifty deals a million times before, if the corruption charges had any truth in them. Following in her father's footsteps, she thought to herself! A strong ominous feeling came over her, and her right eyelid began to twitch. The old Chinese saying "The left eye twitches before fortune; the right one before disaster" came into her head, but it was all a bit too late. By this time she was at the bank. She swallowed hard and entered as calmly as she could.

Within minutes the bank transaction was complete. She now just had to make the phone call, tell them the money was in the prescribed account, and pick up her certificate from the van. Dead easy, she thought.

On the phone, her contacts confirmed that the money had been cabled through and told her where the van would be parked. The instructions seemed clear and the spot easy to reach. When she got there, however, she saw no van. Her heart began to race as she was overcome with panic. Then she found the van, parked just around the corner from where she'd been told it would be. Lili began to run, partly from fear that the van would leave, partly from wanting to get everything over and done with as soon as possible. Traffic lights changed from red to green, and cars moved forward as if in a race. She ran across the street at the first opportunity. Reaching the van, she was handed the certificate, and before she could even acknowledge the giver, the van was gone, joining the race of cars into the distance. Lili had her certificate and the forgers their money. Lili's story is just another side street of capitalism in China's winding road to economic prosperity.

Visit the Forbidden City, take a leisurely stroll in the labyrinth of *hutongs*, or go for a ride on a rickshaw in the vicinity of the Drum and Bell Towers, we are told by the travel books as they list the top-five "must-do" activities in Beijing. This is Beijing, Lonely Planet (the guidebook publisher) style, a capital that allows tourists to imagine themselves exploring the Far East in the same way Marco Polo did some eight centuries earlier. Today visitors can join one of the numerous Marco Polo tours of China or simply pick up a guidebook. All of them will be in search of the magnificent, exotic, and grandiose "old Beijing." Following the itineraries of their guidebooks, tourists will be awestruck by the Forbidden City, overwhelmed by the size of Tiananmen Square, and captivated by the beauty and serenity of the Summer Palace. They will breathe deeply as they take in the splendor of the Temple of Heaven and perhaps even feel enlightened after a trip to the Yonghegong (Lama Temple). Between such landmarks, the guidebooks advise, visitors should take a walk through the alleyways of Houhai and soak up the tranquillity of a "lost" old Beijing. Culinary experiences include the obligatory Peking roast duck at the famous but inexpensive Quanjude Restaurant, Muslim kebabs and ethnic dancing at the Xinjiang Red Rose Restaurant, Tibetan tea at Makye Ame, and a taste of street food in the Wangfujing Street of Snacks. And, just in case their stomachs are not up to such exotic fare, there is always the suburb of Sanlitun, where they can find Western food, Western bars, and lots of fellow Western travelers and ex-pats. There they can sit outside on the tree-lined pavement, drinking, smoking, and flirting into the small hours, or go to a rave or dance party.

54   The Forbidden City: the "authentic" Beijing?

Chinese guidebooks offer a slightly different Beijing. They, too, focus on the not-to-be-missed sites, such as the Forbidden City and Temple of Heaven. They, too, advise a trip to Tiananmen Square and into Mao's mausoleum, with a chance to see the embalmed corpse of the man who changed modern China. Like their Western counterparts, they recommend the purchase of some Mao memorabilia, whether it be a tiepin or a set of chopsticks. Nevertheless, their advice is proffered in a different framework—the framework of nationhood. Chineseness is a key element in the narrative formulations. Hence, Tiananmen Square becomes the site of nation rather than of the incident of 4 June 1989; the Forbidden City and the Two Towers signs of the nation's past greatness. Nevertheless, these guidebooks, too, offer a form of romantic exotica. "Visit the Roman-style architecture of the Wangfujing Cathedral or tour the Baroque-style Xuanwumen Cathedral," they suggest. "Take the tour at night, for it is only then at its most romantic." The West in the East becomes the site of a reverse exoticism. Romanticized and aestheticized, the European imperialist imposition of architectural forms upon China in the late nineteenth century has yielded a positive perspective of the exciting romantic architectural possibilities enabled by the mixture of East and West.

The European-Chinese architecture once politicized by the Maoists stands today, in the guidebook narratives, as no more than an imagined romance. Visited by hundreds of Chinese tourists, the humiliated China of yesteryear has become a China that is seen to have grown and prospered through such interactions. It grows, however, only when the nation has power, and it is when the Chinese guidebooks direct tourists through the Yuanmingyuan, or Garden of Perfect Brightness, that this aspect of the tale is highlighted.

Burned, sacked, and looted by British and French colonial forces in 1860, the Yuanmingyuan was left in ruins. Soldiers were said to have destroyed and vandalized what they did not steal.[9] Although

55   The Baroque-style Xuanwumen Cathedral.

these ruins may now play host to laughing children's games of hide-and-seek, for adult Chinese the destruction of this park is no laughing matter. It plays a crucial role in a nationalist iconography that highlights the need to be strong by playing upon a history of humiliation and weakness. Rendered as a wound inflicted on every Chinese, Yuanmingyuan and the role of the "evil Westerner" is a centerpiece of Chinese guidebooks.

The books use this anti-Western sentiment not to repoliticize the nation, but to reinforce a feeling of loss. No ordinary Chinese had ever seen this place before it was set ablaze and wrecked. A once-secret garden, hidden from the common people for hundreds of years, is now open and visible but only as relic, its magnificent European-style architecture created by the Chinese emperor now but a few rocks and a memory. Chinese tourists who visit this ruin feel a sense of tragic romanticism that will stay with them until nightfall, the best time, their guidebooks tell them, to venture into an area northwest of the Forbidden City known as Houhai.

"You promised me a better price for these couple of girls," complains the businessman as he embraces two prostitutes in one of Houhai's bars while talking to their pimp on a cell phone. They leave the bar and walk alongside the lake, one on either side of their drunken client, who is wearing a big smile. The seaminess of Houhai these days contrasts sadly with the tranquil lake setting once beloved by Chinese royalty and literati. Houhai has become a suburb of bars and restaurants and crowds of drinkers and funseekers. It isn't anything like Amsterdam, but neither is it as it was in dynastic days, when it offered intellectual inspiration and a site of reflection for eager young scholars, members of the imperial family, and the literati. Houhai today, my Chinese friend says as he sighs and shakes his head, is a fallen angel. At night this former site of dynastic scholarly peace is now the heart of Beijing's decadent nightlife. And it is here, with voyeuristic delight, that both the Western and Chinese guidebooks converge in saccharine romanticism.

Two tales of this city, two parallel yet distinct narratives, end up at the same nightclub in Houhai. Grappling with the same complexities, Chinese guidebooks foster a melancholy romanticism about the past that builds into a sense of connection between Chineseness and greatness. Echoing the view that the twenty-first century is China's, they suggest a nation that is on its way to reclaiming its rightful status in the world. It is the narrative of Tiananmen Square at half-past four in the morning, repeated endlessly at each site and each monument. In a parallel narrative, Western guidebooks offer up a romanticized Orientalist version of Beijing. They may recommend the same sites as the Chinese guidebooks, but the visions they promote belong to a different world, one inhabited by wannabe successors to Marco Polo. Of course, a Marco Polo transported to today's Beijing will find a very different place. He will choke on exhaust fumes and be exasperated by the endless traffic jams; he may also wonder at the staggering growth of the city and stare in awe at its new monuments. But invariably his desire will be drawn back toward a Beijing of old. And once that becomes his focus, cynicism will turn to romanticism; not the romanticism of Chineseness, but of great civilizations past.

Humbled when faced with the grandeur of the imperial palaces and gates, he will smell anew the exotic and pungent odors from restaurants such as Haiwanju. He may venture to "old Beijing" by rickshaw and wander into a labyrinth of *hutongs*, now a "conservation zone," that gives the impression of being much larger than it actually is. But when this latter-day Marco Polo stops at an intersection, reality bites: cars, buses, and trucks, construction projects, vast supermarkets, and eye-boggling skyscrapers.

This is a city that allows foreigners and Chinese alike to live in their own dreams, but only for a little while. Just around the corner there is something that will confound them, always something to cast doubt on the "authentic" Beijing that everyone is striving to see. Whether it's the replica Tiananmen Gate, the pirated CD, the

56   The Forbidden City shrouded in scaffolding while it is rebuilt.

tourist-industry-created "old Beijing," or the smells and flavors of Haiwanju, authenticity is hard to find and harder to pin down. The city is, in actuality, merely an anthology of descriptions whose truthfulness gets lost every time one travels to seek truth from facts. As Italo Calvino explains in *Invisible Cities:*

> The city is redundant: it repeats itself so that something will stick in the mind.
>
> Memory is redundant: it repeats signs so that the city can begin to exist.[10]

There is an age-old dogma in Beijing that outsiders are hard-working and contented, whereas the locals are dreamy and ambitious. Industrious outsiders cannot live without aspiring Beijingers in this city that is being constantly remade. The uneasy coexistence of these two groups has shaped Beijing into an extraordinary habitat. If London and New York help define Britain and America yet remain a world unto themselves, in this respect they resemble Beijing in relation to all of China. There are four million registered migrants in this city, and an equal number of "locals" who would name their hometown as somewhere else. It is the diversity and striking contrasts that distinguish Beijing from the rest of the country. It is a capital in transit, of transients, and yet it still references itself in terms of tradition. It is an ancient city, yet one still in the making. The idea of "old Beijing" may well be mythical, but it is nevertheless woven into the new plotline of city development. In a migrant city like Beijing, the pure "Beijing species" has become a myth, one that is perpetuated by the local residents vis-à-vis temporary guest workers. It is a widely held myth, but a myth no less, and it is in seeing the many versions of the authentic that the power of this myth becomes even more apparent.

6 ART MARKET, MARKET ART

The eternal return . . . It's four o'clock on yet another cold, dark, autumn morning in Beijing, and we are again heading out to join an early-morning crowd. This time, however, our destination is not Tiananmen Square, but a market square called Panjiayuan. Dropped off by cab on a street the driver claims is near the market, we pay the fare and ask for further directions. It's pitch black out here, and we're afraid that once the comforting light of the cab disappears, so, too, will our chances of finding this place.

"Just follow the ghosts," says the driver as he points across the road to a long line of overloaded tricycles. "It's not called the ghost market for nothing!" he laughs. And with that, he turns on the taxi light, hits the accelerator, and disappears down the road into the early dawn. The cab is gone, but the words of its driver linger. As our eyes adjust to the early-morning light, we notice a slowly growing one-way stream of three-wheeled silhouettes across the road. As our night vision improves, and we look beyond what lies in front of us, we no longer see row upon row of shadowy tricycles pedaled by weary traders, but instead glimpse an entire ghost army on the move. The transformation is breathtaking. The marching music of this ghost army is the screeching of tricycle brakes and the squeaking of unoiled chains and pedals; its uniform is the shadow of the night, its war cry the yelling and screaming of drivers, traders, and laborers as they push, pull, and pedal their way forward. Perhaps it is because of these shadowy figures pushing and pulling their wagons under dim and flickering streetlights that it is called a ghost market. Then again, it may have more to do with its history.

One hundred years earlier there might well have been a similar cavalcade of carts, wagons, and tricycles traveling in the moonlight toward a dawn market. In significant ways, however, it would have been a very different market from the one that now takes the name Panjiayuan.

In the final years of Qing dynastic rule, when the aristocracy was on the wane but the power of the merchants was still not

57 On the way to the ghost market.

ascendant, the ghost markets of China came into being. Here two very different, almost antithetical worlds would meet: manners (the aristocrats) and market (the traders). Two economies, one of "face," of gifts, of status ascription, and of symbolic capital, the other a more familiar and more "modern" world of markets and money. Although the aristocrats despised the ethos of trade, they increasingly engaged with it. As power shifted to the merchants and traders, the aristocrats were forced to negotiate their declining status, and the ghost market was one such site of negotiation. It was at the ghost market that the impoverished aristocrat and the newly enriched merchant met face to face. Their trade in things developed into a trade in power.

This was not an easy transition for the gentry to make: the antimercantile sentiment fostered by the Confucian value system left no room for the idea of an aristocratic merchant. Nevertheless, aristocrats, buffeted by the harsh winds of dramatic social and economic change, found themselves with little choice. Their survival was ever more problematic without some direct engagement with commerce. For those who tried and failed, as well as for those who failed to try, there were only the ghost markets. The night became the cloak that hid their shame, the setting of compromise between an increasingly humiliated and impoverished gentry and a newly emerging and triumphant merchant class.

Ghost markets enabled aristocrats to maintain their social face while secretly engaging in that most un-Confucian of activities, commerce. As dynastic rule was overthrown and the Republic struggled to survive, hardship became the norm. As it did, the polite fictions created by the Confucian aristocracy—fictions that included an understanding of the world through affect, through the giving and receiving of face, connections, or *guanxi*, through activities of exchange that required no return but nevertheless connected to some part of a person's "spiritual essence"; in other words, some form of Mauss's gift economy—increasingly gave way to a new mercantile reality. The transparent transactions of the marketplace replaced the opaque transactions of *guanxi,* and as they did, the appeal of the ghost markets was that they lay somewhere in between. Ultimately the ghost markets served as a means of ushering in a new world and undermining an older worldview. A nakedly materialist and desacralized world of trading in things began to replace the "public secrets" that were still tied to an economy of face.

Dynastic China was a world of symbols, of balance, of giving and saving face, of emotional connectedness not just with neighbors but also with the spirit world and the ancestors. Oddly, that world would never entirely fade away. This spirit would live on rather strangely under the guise of the iconoclast—the Chinese Communist Party. Sacrifice for the Party would underpin the politics of commitment that led to the Ten Great Projects. And we have seen that even today this gift economy still has life, although it operates in an almost unrecognizable form in the alleyways of Jiaodaokou. The history of this transforming spirit reasserts itself as we pass through the gates of Panjiayuan into the ghost market.

Today in China there is no longer any shame attached to commerce, and the ghost market of Panjiayuan no longer masks an aristocratic secret. Any secrets traded at Panjiayuan today are Party secrets. Sold by weight, Party documents, "classified" books, journals, and dossiers, are one stop away from the rubbish dumps of Bajiacun. Yet for collectors of Party secrets, they are a gold mine. If one looked hard enough, one might even find Liu Zhengxian's report on Hu Feng. Yet in many cases these purported materials from the Maoist period, and especially the political kitsch—the political posters, the statues, the badges, the Little Red Book—are forgeries. The Mao craze of the 1990s has left its mark; revolutionary kitsch is "in."

Collectors of this material come in droves. They sift through forgeries and pirate editions to uncover the authentic and the original. The political "true believers" of the Mao era have long gone. Now the collectors are the only "true believers" in this market. At the crack of dawn, it is the collectors' flashlights that illuminate items of sale and not the lamps of embarrassed aristocrats or down-at-heel gentry. Yet the fairy lights dancing across the marketplace still endow the site with a certain romance and magic. These days, it is not face but the best bargains and the most authentic wares that keep the lights burning and the traditions of the ghost market alive.

As the gates of Panjiayuan are thrown open, the crowd surges forward. A sudden air of urgency surrounds collectors and dealers alike. The quiet murmur of just seconds before gives way to yelling and screaming. It's like a gold rush—tricycles, carts, trucks, and hundreds of people on foot, all shouting, hurrying, surging, squeezing through the gate and rushing in to occupy a prominent spot. A tricycle hits a cart; there's a momentary tussle, a little swearing; and all the time the weight of people outside pushes inexorably forward. Before six in the morning, this space of free trade is also rent-free, so the usual peasants, merchants, and dealers are joined briefly by amateur traders with no money in their pockets and only a handful of family trinkets in their bags to sell.

Behind the carts and tricycles, like minnows following whales, comes a small army of flashlight-wielding collectors, antique dealers, and connoisseurs. They descend upon what is now claimed to be one of the world's largest flea markets with the spirits of gamblers and the desires of alchemists.[1] They come to this place every weekend to chance their luck. These latter-day Taoists are here to turn trash into treasure. If anyone can do it, they can. Indeed, at half-past four in the morning the magic of their enthusiasm seems able to turn darkness into daylight. Welcome to their fairyland.

As the potential buyers move eagerly through the bric-a-brac and fakes, their lights flickering across the enclosure, we imagine ourselves back in Bajiacun with Li, his wife, and the plastic bags,

58   Waiting for the gates to open.

panning, just like these more opulent alchemists, for wealth and treasure; or back in Wudaokou with young Wang panning through jumbled collections of saw-gash CDs in search of the "real stuff"; or back in Wudaokou with Yao Yao, sitting in his new café, sipping coffee, checking out women, and dreaming his impossible dream.

The pushing and shoving of the Panjiayuan crowd shatters these visions. Yet our thoughts do not settle on the "here and now" of Panjiayuan. Instead our daydreaming turns to the aristocrats who, like us, must have been pushed and shoved in this marketplace as the world they knew crumbled before them. For those whose dreams have never been fulfilled, as well as for those whose dream world is fast disappearing, life is lived as paradox.

These figures of the threshold are always caught somewhere between the worlds of money and magic.[2] They are dreamers, collectors, and connoisseurs when they are not being gold diggers, con artists, and gamblers. And the disparate spirits of these figures are here in Panjiayuan as they scramble in their hundreds through the gates in the predawn light on their way to con or be conned, to dig and to pan, to find the "real," the authentic, the genuine among the endless rows of fakes. They are buoyed by endless stories of ghosts, magic, and miracles; stories of real discoveries, authentic finds, and genuine success. In Panjiayuan, tales of this sort are the stuff of urban legend.

There is the story of an antique dealer who unknowingly sold a million-dollar Yuan Dynasty vase for less than ten Chinese dollars. There is another tale of someone buying a pile of documents, Bajiacun style, by weight, and finding amid this purchased "trash" hundreds of rare photographs and negatives by a famous photographer. Then there is the story of an information-technology executive from Zhongguancun, Zhao Qingwei, who bought a pile of old materials about the Cultural Revolution by weight only to find they were far weightier than he'd imagined. Inside the case were hundreds of rare documents, books, and photographs of that period. So rare were they that they would later be put on exhibition in Beijing.[3] Perhaps the most spectacular tale of all is one involving the sale of a 100-kilogram fossil that was later identified as a priceless five-million-year-old bone from the head of a mammoth.[4]

Urban legends like these keep Panjiayuan in business because they whet the appetites of collectors and keep the crowds coming. As we join these throngs and observe the haggling, the inspection of goods, the spin and the counterspin of this early-morning marketplace, we discover that the traders are well aware of their market, their "marks," and these tales; all they have to do is to make their goods seem like the next legendary treasure.

Old Xu, who trades in antique furniture, does just that. He has traveled all night from his rural factory in Hebei to make it to the market by dawn. His truck is loaded down with "antiques." His factory takes ancient things and "restores" them, yet his restoration technique destroys the very thing he is restoring. His technique is a form of dismemberment. He points to an antique temple chair and tells us how he distributed its legs among four other chairs, thus turning all four into new "authentic" antiques! These parts taken to make a different whole are components of a metonymic race for profit that, on the one hand, throws in doubt the very idea of the real, the authentic, and the genuine, yet, on the other, exists only because it valorizes it. In a place whose very name, "ghost market," seems to lack a single origin, it is the promise of an authentic original that keeps the lively searching and selling alive. Panjiayuan is clearly a place of paradox.

From traders in antique porcelain to those who trade in the paraphernalia of the Mao years, the significant and the insignificant, the fake and the real, the artistic and the kitsch mix so effectively that even the connoisseur-collectors often find their flashlight beams too weak to detect the difference. Traders, for their part, try to differentiate between connoisseur-collector and rank amateur. In Panjiayuan, traders invent techniques to use their abstract knowledge of these characters to concrete advantage: a wise word here, a knowledgeable glance there, displays of expertise or signs of ignorance—all enable the traders to construct an informal hierarchy of buyers. As it develops, they determine whether to show them fakes or ever-rarer specimens. Traders have the eyes and minds of police detectives, and, as every police detective will tell you, the law is always there to establish the limits on behavior. Panjiayuan is a "game" with its own rules and with limits. In this respect it is an economic version of the stadium crowd: the thrilling intensity of the moment may come from the discovery of a rare find rather than from a winning goal, but in both cases the rules of these games set the limits and help both venues avoid the cycles of violence that politicized intensity can produce. If sport helps draw the sting from politics, so, too, can commerce.

"War is politics by other means," wrote Clausewitz, but even for him, politics was more like a form of commerce. Politics, Clausewitz observed, is merely "a kind of commerce on a larger scale."[5] The marketplace of Panjiayuan is but one small site of this larger-scale endeavor. There traders and collectors may well wage a "war" involving knowledgeability and price, but violence is excluded by one of the key rules of trade. In this respect the marketplace can be thought of as part of what Elias once dubbed the "civilizing process." Marketplace contracts may in time kill off the gift economy, but they also help temper the passions and limit political violence. In this regard, Panjiayuan is one small example of what economic reform has achieved across the whole of China.

If Tiananmen Square at dawn now captures the spirit of the nation, Panjiayuan at dawn is host to the spirit of capitalism. Where Tiananmen might still awaken memories of a socialist political past, Panjiayuan awakens both dreams of future wealth and memories of the dynastic past. Paradoxically, as the gate opens just before dawn, the collectors' flashlights cast a beam on a world in which commerce did not rule. Panjiayuan also brings that world to

59   Mao paraphernalia.

life through sales of statues of Buddhas' heads and Taoist gods, antique paintings and vases, trinkets, jewelry, and "antique" furniture.

Panjiayuan also calls up another spirit world, one manifested in relics of a very different kind: Mao badges, Little Red Books, and classified material from the 1950s and 1960s, and revolutionary posters and statues from the 1960s and 1970s. These increasingly compete with the Buddha heads and antique furniture to offer a world of different Chinese memories. Indeed, Panjiayuan is nothing if not the idea of selling China's past, its memories and its dreams, in a newly commodified form, to a new emerging clientele. In this regard, Panjiayuan offers an experience vastly different from those of ordinary commercial markets.

Most items for sale in Panjiayuan are purchased not for their utility but almost because of their lack of functionality; their renewed value derives from their role as collectors' fetishized objects. They will have a new life or an afterlife in a world in which functionality has yielded to the idea of total possession.[6] The individualized passions of collectors, not the collectivized political passions of the socialist past, form the driving spirit of Panjiayuan.

Thus even when collectors come to Panjiayuan seeking objects with old political associations, they are no longer necessarily a register of political commitment. On the contrary, the passion of collecting completely displaces the passion of politics into a world of everyday and individualized desires. Here in Panjiayuan we witness the aestheticization of politics.

Mao buttons, Mao statues, and all the other assorted paraphernalia of the prereform era are collected not to relive the politics of that era, but to complete "the set." In the process, Mao occupies memory only as an afterlife afterthought. Recasting Mao in this way, as an aesthetic object of reflection rather than as a potent political symbol, may, at this stage, be the only way China can consume its once-revered Chairman. Hemmed in by a Party that still

60   Mao amid the new materialism.

61   Waiting to see Chairman Mao.

avows the Maoist legacy yet retains its legitimacy only by abandoning it in favor of market-based modernization, the merchants of Panjiayuan cut out a small space for trade, selling off pirated Mao statues and fake relics of that era as the genuine article. Perhaps it is because it has to negotiate so much of its trade in relation to the relic, the past, that which has been, that Panjiayuan is called a ghost market. Yet if Mao's ghost still lurks in this marketplace, how much more his presence must haunt a place like Tiananmen Square. Perhaps that is why the issue of authenticity is so much more potent and troubling for that site.

Let us join the line of peasants and workers, women and children, cadres and couples, who have traveled to Tiananmen Square to look at the body of their beloved Chairman. This square, with its symbols of socialism, remains the staging ground of the nation. Have all these people wearing sunglasses, laughing, joking, chatting, and endlessly taking photographs of themselves really come to show their respect, or has this "event" simply become a form of free entertainment? On a day when these Chinese tourist groups are running around the square snapping any background shot in sight, we are lined up like a row of prisoners en route to the dead center. Yet just as this long line of shabbily dressed, sometimes rude, and always loud rural tourists begins to remind us of a Disneyland crowd, along comes a young guy like Jiang Rui.

He is an eighteen-year-old boy from Shenyang who has recently graduated from high school. He has come to Beijing to see his cousin, his sister, and the Chinese capital. He's dreamed all his life of visiting Beijing, and for him, Tiananmen Square is the highlight of that visit. A trip to Tiananmen Square is obligatory, and the Chairman's embalmed corpse is one of the must-sees of any visit to the square.

Jiang Rui is just in front of us in the slow-moving crowd. Just before entering, he is persuaded by the flower vendor to buy a bouquet to place in front of the white marble statue of Mao that stands three meters high in the main hall. After about an hour's wait as the line snakes around and into the building, Jiang finally makes it to the main hall, where he leaves the line and places his bouquet at the foot of the statue of the Chairman. He bows twice in reverence, fixing a solemn gaze upon the enormous statue, and moves on, in tears. By now the crowd has moved slowly forward toward the next room, where Mao's crystal sarcophagus rests. As we move out of the main hall, the vendor who has sold Jiang the flowers comes in and retrieves each of the bouquets strewn across the floor. As we pass by the vendor's stall on our way out, we find Jiang's flowers back in place, awaiting another patriotic soul who wants to leave some tribute to the Great Helmsman. When Jiang sees them, his face falls, tears well up, and he shakes his head in disbelief. "Hey, listen, everyone has to make a buck," explains the flower vendor, clearly uneasy about his own disrespectful actions. This could very well become the new slogan of postreform China. Yet the degree of unease, of sheer embarrassment and discomfort, shown by the vendor as he snatched the flowers away from the foot of Mao's statue is something that many in post-economic-reform China have also felt.

"The Mao image has a charisma of its own. It's still so powerful that the first time I cut up an official portrait of Mao for a collage I felt a pang of guilt, something gnawing away inside me. Other people, in particular other Chinese, may well feel the same. As long as this 'power to intimidate' exists, I will continue to do Mao."[7]

So said the New York–based Chinese artist Zhang Hongtu back in the 1980s as he took a knife to an official portrait of the Chairman in what was then a radical act in the very early days of the avant-garde art scene in China. These days, any artist who wants a radical, dissident, and different image is pretty much doing some version of the same thing: cutting up Mao, cutting up socialism, cutting up radicalism. Mao may no longer be the favorite cut-up boy of the avant-garde, but parodic references to his era are everywhere. Indeed, even the location of the avant-garde art colony of Beijing in an old socialist factory called 798 bespeaks this era. Here Maoism is alive, but only as Andy Warhol's version of the Chairman on show.

Just look at the artwork of a onetime resident of 798, Sui Jianguo. His sculpture *The Sleeping Mao* tried to overcome Zhang's "gnawing" feeling by secularizing the Chairman. "[Now] I understand that Mao was just a man too. He was not a God. God doesn't sleep, but man does. Mao changed my path when I was young. But now I should take charge of my own life."[8]

Sui's desire to make and sell Mao was part of the same self-exploration that informed Zhang Hongtu's work, but by the time Sui was molding his Maos in Factory 798, many others there were also doing Mao or other parodies of China's socialist past. Indeed, so many were doing Mao that it became hard to determine where self-exploration ended and marketization began. Essentially, such artwork became not only a parody on Mao but also a parody on itself. Works that turned the horror of the Mao years into a surreal "critique" became big-ticket items in the Western rather than the Chinese art market, and at the forefront of this boom was 798.

No other place makes a more splendid backdrop to a satire on "China and globalization" than Factory 798. Here avant-garde art galleries and old socialist work units sit cheek by jowl in the red-light district of contemporary Chinese avant-garde art. Fortuitously connected by yellow, violet, and sky-blue pipelines that add color to the austere Bauhaus-style architecture, they join two worlds that are at opposite ends of the political spectrum.

A giant brick chimney towers over the landscape, affirming the centrality of industry, a relic of an era when the Socialist Centralized Economic Plan and state-owned enterprises were all-powerful. The political unity that was once forged in the factory is

62   Maoism 798 style.

63   The marketing of art.

frowned upon here these days, although revolutionary politics itself has become a hot theme for shows and sales. Fame may be dismissed as unimportant by these grungy-looking budding artists, but it's every artist's ambition. Concealing this desire for material comfort is a crucial part of the art of being a (con) artist. Spray-painted graffiti proclaiming a psychopolitics of dissent now overlay Cultural Revolution slogans on the walls of Factory 798.

Time for afternoon tea, 798 style! Gallery owners, fashion designers, art aficionados, and the artists themselves congregate in sumptuous surrounds—redesigned warehouses of the old socialist-era industry. Sipping their lattes or drinking Chardonnays, they have cultivated quite a taste for European food thanks to their Western patrons' continuing investment and support. The result is that 798 is no longer a grungy, decaying industrial site but a jewel of urban renewal, full of cafés, bars, and restaurants that feed the up-and-coming Chinese artists a Western buyers' diet. A few doors down from the faux industrialism of the art colony is the real thing. Genuinely grungy work-unit laborers have just finished their plain noodle soup topped with some ultrathin pork slices in a tiny, dirty workers' café. The noodle shop has no doors, no air conditioning, and it is clearly a place that health inspectors have missed. Nevertheless, the workers seem as devoted to demolishing their noodles as the artists do to parodying their industrial life. Indeed, the laborers and artists have little in common except a somewhat misconstrued notion of collaboration that underpins the 798 "work of art" colonies project. The only collaboration around, however, seems to be between factory bosses who rent out warehouse space at exorbitant rates and avant-garde artists who return the favor by spoofing the worldview of their landlords. In an ironic twist, it is the wealthy avant-garde artistic dissidents who are saving this last remaining example of the socialist-state-planned work unit from extinction.

Long gone are the days when Factory 798 could rely upon the

64   Yan Lei's *Color Wheels*.

state. In its heyday, 798 was a huge place, making parts for the socialist plan. Munitions for the military, electronic components for radio and communications systems, and power for the leadership compound at Zhongnanhai—these were the key products of Factory 798 of the Central Plan. With economic reform, that comfortable existence gave way to a new economic reality. Like all state-run enterprises, 798 was told to make money. Communist cadres just out of earshot of Maoism were possibly not the best economic advisers to lead 798 into this new future, and what followed was testimony to this fact.

The factory tried to become the dumpling king of Beijing, but the city wasn't buying. It also tried a range of other sideline businesses, but all of them drained rather than augmented the factory's increasingly scarce resources. Before too long, 798's bank account was turning redder than a Maoist political campaign; so when the academy of art needed cheap temporary studio and warehouse space back in 1995 while its buildings were being refurbished, 798 was quick to rent out its unused warehouses. After the academy moved in, other artists started renting space from the factory and setting up their own private studios there.

"Low rent, lots of space, an open atmosphere and an artistic vibe attracted me to move in here," recalled Xu Yong, the president of the 798 Art Space Center back in 2004.[9] In those days rents were cheap. When the academy moved in back in 1995, rental space was reportedly twelve dollars (Chinese) per square meter; by 2004 it was sixty dollars. Since then the price has more than doubled.[10] With growing demand, prices increased, and the central planners, Party cadres, and socialist industries of 798 found their unlikely savior—the avant-garde art industry! Long burdened by debt stemming from the huge benefits it had to pay retired and laid-off workers, by 2002, as a result of the revenue stream from shop and gallery owners and from artists who rented space there, the factory found that its fifty-million-dollar financial black hole had shrunk to twenty million.[11]

By this time, trendy cafés, hip bars, and up-market restaurants were joining funky art spaces, bookshops, and galleries to make 798 the chicest place in town. Thus, by the time the academy left the compound in 2000, the hottest new products coming off the assembly lines of Factory 798 were café lattes, Italian pasta, and avant-garde Chinese art. And when the artists weren't joining their clients and friends sipping Chardonnays or coffee, they were back in their studios making postmodern art for a Western market that couldn't seem to get enough of it and was willing to pay top dollar for it.

Artwork coming out of 798 doesn't so much aestheticize politics as marketize it. It's Panjiayuan with artistic pretensions, but, unlike the ghost market, 798 caters not to a Chinese palate but to a Western one. All too often, it offers an artistic rendition of what the West wants to believe constitutes authentic political dissent: parodies of socialism accompanied by the appropriate degree of "Chineseness" just to give it that necessary touch of authenticity.

It was as a result of the profitability of this genre that the old Socialist Realist style taught in the art academies gave way, in 798, to what some would call "cynical realism," while political art was transformed into political pop. Add to this a touch of what is now called Gaudy art, and the picture is complete. Yet this picture is deceptive. The avant-garde art scene may present itself as a picture of political dissent, but it does so by saving one of the key industries of the old socialist industrial era. In other words, the very system the contemporary artists critique is now being subsidized by their rents! This is not the only paradox of the 798 art world.

Flying the flag of dissent, the avant-garde artists mock the Mao era. Instead of a rifle the soldier now holds a paintbrush; instead of a Maoist slogan there is a play on Maoist words. Nevertheless, when it comes to political matters, these same artists express their concerns for the proletariat and the lower strata of society to the assembled Western media. This little bit of Maoist concern, however, has less to do with any redolent radical politics, some suggest, than with the power of Western tastes and sensibilities to shape the Chinese contemporary art market. Consequently, in press conferences contemporary artists will employ a version of the old Maoist notion of the mass line "from the masses to the masses" to show compassion and respect for the lower strata of society while the peasant-workers they employ follow a well-rehearsed script, only this time they do it for the artists rather than for the Central Committee. "They are workers too," say the peasant-workers about the artists. "We totally comprehend their labor."[12] Thus, in the language of faux Maoism the artists package a form of Mao that becomes marketable to Western buyers because it at once shows contempt for the Maoist past yet repeats Maoism's once-oft-expressed concern for the people.

Yan Lei is one such artist, yet he is also a parody of them all. He never touches the canvas but instead hires a group of peasant-workers to do his painting. More a graphic designer working with peasant-workers than an artist, Yan's dazzling and mesmeric work, such as his famous *Color Wheels*, was created without his lifting a brush to make a single stroke. Instead, peasant-workers beavered away, painting by numbers organized on the basis of a prearranged color code. Each worker would paint his allocated section of the wheel; then the work was moved to the next workbench for the next worker to paint his or her section. It is classic assembly-line stuff. Yan would end up hiring ten workers for his factory, and the result was a highly prolific output of one "authentic" Yan Lei "original" wheel per day.

Yan's production techniques are part of his long-standing strident critique of the Chinese avant-garde art scene. The artists' self-importance and sense of their own individual genius irritated Yan, who wanted to prick their artistic pretensions by showing the fraudulent quality of their work. The *Color Wheels* are his latest attempt; his earliest and most controversial effort, the *Invitation Letter*, was far more pointed and shot him to fame in 1997.

Concocted with co-conspirator Hong Hao, the *Invitation Letter* was called performance art, but it wasn't Hong and Yan who performed. Instead, they attempted to dupe some famous artists and curators in the Chinese avant-garde art scene by sending out fake invitation letters to participate in the internationally renowned art exhibition Documenta, in Kassel, Germany. Faking Documenta letterhead and signing the invitations using the name Mr. Ielnay Oahgnoh—which is simply Hong Hao and Yan Lei written backward—they sent the invitation to some of China's top artists and critics. There was an unseemly scramble to take up the offer, but no one could find Mr. Ielnay Oahgnoh. The search for him became a performance in itself, and before the fraud was exposed, the avant-garde elite had already exposed themselves.

Bragging about their international fame and chasing obsequiously after this foreign invitation, the artists and critics displayed a desire for international recognition above all else. Needless to say, once the fraud was exposed, the Chinese contemporary art world was incensed by the *Invitation Letter* "performance artwork." Thus a couple of con artists became famous themselves for criticizing other con artists.

Yan Lei's work is all about debunking the pretensions, the fraud, and the dubious methodological claims of the Chinese avant-garde art scene. "Strictly speaking, I'm not an artist," says Yan, "but since 1996 I have done some works relating to contemporary art issues. I didn't choose a fixed pattern or medium where these issues would be taken up. Instead, I did these things because I was bored with the traditional means of expression and I began to question the essentially modernistic taste that claimed to be at the heart of contemporary art." After his performance-based venture,

65   Pandaman demonstrates how to "Oppose Violence!"

Yan Lei started producing his own artwork of "everyday life," beginning with *Second-Hand Shop* (1999).

With *Second-Hand Shop*, Yan Lei not only invited audiences into his life; he also allowed them to purchase his belongings at discounted prices. "Shifting his own life space" to "test new experiences that the metropolis provides for individual vision, space and psychology" was how he described it.[13]

Of course, not every Factory 798 artist is as enamored of the artistic possibilities of real life as Yan Lei. Some of these artists go for a more surreal rather than real-life performance.

Pandaman is one of them. Humorous, irreverent, and often pretty silly, Pandaman enacts a politics of the absurd, a political satire on seriousness. In a place that takes national symbols so seriously, Pandaman's antics pack a punch. Tracing his (mis)adventures through a series of sight gags captured as captioned photographs, Pandaman travels the world exposing absurdities in rhetoric and life.

When it comes to exposing the hypocrisies of antiterrorist rhetoric, Pandaman has few rivals. Screaming out "Oppose violence!" he beats up a terrorist villain. "Would you mind my smoking?" Pandaman asks Panda as they sit in conversation. "Would you mind my extinction?" replies the poker-faced bear. "It seems you still believe in true love, don't you?" Pandaman suggests to a gay European couple sunning themselves on a public lawn. In a nearby toilet cubicle Pandaman "interviews" a couple of semiconscious junkies who've just shot up. They turn to Pandaman and say with straight faces, "The crime rate is too high. We worry about that."

Wryly and often discordantly, the absurd rubs shoulders with the politically explosive. When Pandaman returns home to China, Panda joins him on a shopping expedition to a new and expensive department store selling discounted panda dolls. Holding a magnifying glass to one eye while cradling Panda in his arms, Pandaman

66   Pandaman and Panda examine toy bears for authenticity.

and bear stare down in shocked disbelief at a pile of discounted toys. Then Panda breaks the silence: "Are they clones of me?" he says in an anxious manner. No, replies Pandaman Zhao, taking a closer look with his magnifying glass; "They are fakes!"

Yet as we look down with him upon this pile of identical pandas for sale, and then look up at the panda he cradles, we just know that Pandaman, like us, has no way of knowing the real from the clone or the clone from the fake. We are in fact back to dilemmas about authenticity; back in Panjiayuan scrambling with flashlights looking for the real, lining up at the Chairman Mao Memorial Hall to view the "real" mummified corpse of the dead Chairman, looking at a replica of Tiananmen Gate, searching for authentic symbols of "old Beijing" during a tricycle tour of Jiaodaokou, eating the authentic "old Beijing" cuisine, or looking through a pile of toy panda bears. Symbols of nation, of city, of people are reproduced as artifacts, becoming what Jean Baudrillard calls the "vengeance of the dead."[14] In this town, objects of national belonging, things that bind the crowd to Tiananmen Square at dawn, things that bring pride in the idea of Chineseness are all reproduced in a sustained process that leads to both the original's and the replica's appearing artificial.

Here, in this world of the phony real, the faked replica, and the inauthentic clone, the idea of a regeneration of the imaginary leads us to think, claims Baudrillard, of the "waste-treatment plant."[15] We are back with sorting the good from the bad plastic bag in Bajiacun. We are, in fact, looking at the regeneration of the national imaginary, and finding in its rubbish heaps a grotesque reflection of Beijing's fast-paced disposable commodified world. Yet when it comes to the regeneration of the imaginary we are also, somewhat more oddly, drawn back into Tiananmen Square. Once the heart of a project to memorialize a China liberated by socialism, Tiananmen Square has now become the epicenter of Chinese nationalism. It is the ground shared both by the "old Beijing" of the socialist era and the "New Beijing," perhaps best captured in the figure of an Olympic city. Yet there is little doubt which is in the ascendant.

"New Beijing" is of course one half of the Olympic slogan "New Beijing, New Olympics." It flags a new city sensibility and a new form of political campaigning. If "old Beijing" was all about "the masses," about striving to politicize and mobilize through socialist ideas, "New Beijing" is all about money and advertising. Yet there is always, still, something of the political campaign in any advertising blitz, and one built around the Olympics is little different. Quirkily, it is Pandaman who points to the latent political element of the campaign when he is spurred by a type of national pride to elect himself the unofficial spokesperson for the 2008 Beijing Olympics and then jog out of the gates of Factory 798 and take the message of a new "New Beijing, New Olympics" to the world. Dressed as an Olympic runner, Zhao Bandi, alias Pandaman, carries only a toy panda on his shoulder and a plastic Olympic torch in his hand; yet he is off to conquer the world. A twenty-seven-minute video shows us Pandaman's worldwide exploits, inspired by an emotional nationalist surge that enveloped Beijing when it was announced that it was to be the host city for the 2008 Olympics. Pandaman took the slogan of the game seriously and with the words "One World, One Dream" raised the (plastic) Olympic torch like a cudgel and set off on a mission. Parodying the path of the official Olympic torchbearer, he runs through the main streets of Europe where police have blocked off roads to enable his passage, and into the backstreets of Beijing, where kids, screaming, laughing, and shouting, block his way. Still running, Pandaman arrives in a Beijing stadium and lights the eternal flame to the welcoming dances of the "Pandaettes" and the rapturous applause of thousands of mask-wearing panda people.

The panda crowd is rapturous, caught in the electric moment that brings on a swelling of national pride. This is a parody of that feeling captured at dawn in Tiananmen Square as the flag goes up and the hearts of the Chinese visitors swell with pride. It's a parody of that feeling that was recruited and employed in the political campaigns of the Maoist past. It's a spirit of politics, harnessed this time not for socialist political ends but as a means to turn the tables on an advertising campaign that proclaims "New Beijing, New Olympics" on a new groundswell of national unity and national pride. Through Pandaman the vanity of nation is opened to devastating parody. "A joke is a playful judgment," wrote Freud, a judgment that brings to the surface "suppressed subsidiary thoughts."[16]

The thoughts that Pandaman's Olympic tour spoke to are, however, never far from the surface, and they are mainly bellicose.

"I tried to avoid buying Japanese lenses for my camera, but I had no choice," complains our young photographer as he changes the lens of his camera for a close-up shot of Pandaman calling for a panda invasion of Taiwan. "If we ever use military force to take back Taiwan, I'll be the first to volunteer," says the computer technician fixing one of our overworked machines in Beijing. "I'm the only son, but I don't care," he adds. There is a kaleidoscope of views about nation, and there are parallel times with parallel lives being lived. When it comes to Chineseness and the shared assurance about China's future, however, there is a sense of unity and purpose. The twenty-first century will be China's, and Beijing will be its showpiece; the people here will tell you as much. It is, in fact, already Beijing's time. So welcome to "New Beijing," and welcome to the future.

NOTES

ADDITIONAL SOURCES

ACKNOWLEDGMENTS

INDEX

NOTES

1 THE SQUARE

1 The ceremony existed in the past but not on the same scale. It started in December 1982 when the task of raising the flag was transferred from the People's Liberation Army to the National Flag-Raising Brigade of the People's Armed Police. At this time it was a simple ritual performed by three soldiers daily on the basis of a timetable formulated by the Beijing Astrology Station. In April 1991, when a nationalist agenda produced the Law on the National Flag, the Beijing city government ordered the expansion and enhancement of the ceremony for patriotic purposes. Its current elaborate and ritualistic form was in place by May 1991. For details see Jia Yingting, *Tiananmen* (Beijing: China Commercial Press, 1988), 136–140.

2 Liang Sicheng, quoted in Chang-tai Hung, "Revolutionary History in Stone: The Making of a Chinese National Monument," *China Quarterly* 166 (June 2001), 460.

3 For the most detailed discussion of the controversy surrounding the redevelopment of this central city shopping mall see Anne-Marie Broudehoux, *The Making and Selling of Post-Mao Beijing* (London: Routledge, 2004), 120.

4 Wang Jun, *The Record of Beijing* (Taipei: Gao tan wen hua shi ye you xian gong si, 2005), 53.

5 Chen Guanzhong, *Bohemian China* (Hong Kong: Oxford University Press, 2004), 5.

6 Song Xiaoxia, "Tiyan chengshi" (To experience the city), *Ershiyi Shiji Shuangyuekan* (Twenty-first Century), no. 43 (October 1997), 101.

7 On the views of Chinese that their nation will be the power of the twenty-first century see Chen Xiaoming, "Wenhuaminzu zhuyi dexingqi" (The rise of "cultural nationalism"), ibid., no. 39 (February 1997), 35. The Chinese have an exceptionally upbeat view of their future; in a recent survey asking people in eighty countries whether the future for theirs was bright or bleak, a majority in only three countries answered positively, and of those the Chinese were far and away the most positive: a staggering 83 percent of respondents

said that their country's future was bright. See Carole Cadwalladr, "The Great Leap Forward [Dispatches]," *Observer Magazine*, 21 January 2007, 35.

8 Banknotes had been released earlier, on the eve of the Communist takeover. These so-called Series 1 notes were used by the Communists when they entered various cities. For further details see Helen Wang, "Mao on Money," *East Asian Journal* 1, no. 2 (2003), 92.

9 Chen Gan, quoted in Wang, *The Record of Beijing*, 53.

10 This decision was taken by the Chinese People's Political Consultative Conference on its final day, 30 September 1949.

11 The CCP was not the first to try to alter the city's cosmology. The city was first reoriented in the early years of the Republic. In his talk "Beijing Reoriented, an Olympic Undertaking" (27 June 2007), Geremie R. Barmé pointed out that Yuan Shikai, first president and near emperor, reoriented the city by organizing a military parade from east to west at his inauguration. This was followed in the Republic and during the Japanese occupation with the building of the new gates Jianguomen and Fuxingmen, both of which reflect their Republican-era national sentiment and the sense of "national revival." Hence the Communists were not the first, although they were easily the most successful.

12 Mao's calligraphy was given pride of place. While it reads "Eternal Glory to the People's Heroes" *(renmin yingxiong yongchui buxiu)* to a mainland Chinese, in Taiwan the expression *yongchui buxiu* is colloquial for "permanent hard-on"! Zhou Enlai's calligraphy employed a much longer quote from Mao Zedong written in the style of a poem that repeats in each stanza the "eternal glory" of each of the historical peoples who participated in the struggle for national liberation. Each of the moments of eternal glory mentioned in the quotation correlates with one of the marble carvings.

13 Hung, "Revolutionary History in Stone," 461.

14 Ibid., 468.

15 Mao Zedong, "On New Democracy," in *Selected Works*, vol. 2 (Peking: Foreign Languages Press, 1977), 354.

16 Benedict Anderson in his seminal text *Imagined Communities* (London: Verso, 1983), 17.

17 Ibid.

18 This is the Marx of the *Communist Manifesto*. For details of the panels in English, see Wu Hung, *Remaking Beijing: Tiananmen Square and the Creation of a Political Space* (Chicago: Chicago University Press, 2005), 32–34; and Hung, "Revolutionary History in Stone," 466 ff.

19 The National Theater was never built owing to lack of funds, which also accounted for the empty interior in the Revolutionary Museum; Zou Denong, *Zhongguo xiandai jianzhu shi* (A history of contemporary architecture in China) (Beijing: China Machine Press, 2003), 67. On the Ten Great Projects see Beijing guihua weiyuanhui, Beijing chengshi guihua xuehui (Beijing Planning Commission and Beijing Municipal Planning Association), *Beijing shida jianshu sheji* (Ten prominent buildings) (Tianjin: Tianjin University Press, 2002), 161–181.

20 Quoted in Wu, *Remaking Beijing*, 23.

21 See Shu Jun, *Tiananmen guangchang lishi dangan* (Historical archives related to Tiananmen Square) (Beijing: Press of the School of the Chinese Communist Party, 1998), 61–62; Jia, *Tiananmen*, 117–118.

22 "Draw things according to me" could also be rendered as "Do what I say," for in the Chinese expression *zhao woshuo de hua* the last word, *hua*, is pronounced in exactly the same way but written in two different ways. One of these means "to speak," the other "to draw." For further details, see Jin Shoushen, *Beijing de chuangshuo* (Beijing Legends) (Beijing: Beijing Press, 2002), 1–8.

23 Often portrayed as an *enfant terrible* trickster, Nezha is found in a number of classical fictional works such as *Xiyouji*, or *Journey to the West*, which Americans may know through the monkey king. Nezha is typically depicted as having eight arms and flying in the sky with a wheel of fire under each foot, a golden loop, and a "cosmic ring." He has an impulsive and mischievous character, sometimes unforgivably rebellious, though he rarely appears as entirely villainous. In some accounts, he is prescient and directive.

24 Wang Jun, "The Axis: Life Sources of Beijing," in Yin Lichuan et al., *Beijing zai beijing shengcun de yibaige li you* (100 reasons to enjoy Beijing) (Taipei: Dakuai wenhua Publishing House, 2005), 3.

25 In fact a 1973 survey of the palace revealed that there were only 8,704 rooms in the palace compound; *Gu Gong*, Part 2: *Shengshi de* *wuji* (The roof of the world), CCTV television series, Beijing Palace Museum and China Central Television Station, 2005.

26 Li Zhisui, *The Private Life of Chairman Mao* (New York: Random House, 1994), 14.

27 Ibid., 23.

28 Katherine Verdery, *The Political Lives of Dead Bodies* (New York: Columbia University Press, 2000), 143, n. 127; Vladislav Todorov, *Red Square Black Square: Organon for Revolutionary Imagination* (Albany: SUNY, 1995), 133–134.

2 THE MAP

1 James Ferguson and Akhil Gupta, "Spatializing States: Toward an Ethnography of Neoliberal Governmentality," *American Ethnologist* 29, no. 4 (2002), 981.

2 Michel de Certeau, *Practice of Everyday Life*, trans. Steven F. Randall (Berkeley: University of California Press, 1998), 92.

3 Timothy Mitchell, *Colonising Egypt* (New York: Cambridge University Press, 1988), 24.

4 Ferguson and Gupta, "Spatializing States," 963.

5 Robin Pogrebin, "Embracing Koolhaas's Friendly Skyscraper," *New York Times,* 16 November 2006, E1.

6 The guiding principles of contemporary Chinese architecture make an impossible set of demands. Buildings must express the cultural tradition *(wenhua chuantong)*, feature local characteristics *(difang fengge)*, and capture the spirit of the time *(shidai jingshen)*. For further details on architectural guidelines and restrictions in Beijing, see "Guowuyuan dui Beijing zhongti guihua pifu" (Permission for Beijing's overall plan from State Council), State Memorandum, Beijing, 1993. Typical effects of these demands include the New Dongan Market in the Wangfujing shopping district, the Customs Building and the Women's Federation Building on the Avenue of Eternal Peace, and the new Western Railway Station in the southwest area of Beijing.

7 "National Grand Theatre of China: An Opening Curtain of Laminated Glass," http://www.dupont.com/safetyglass/lgn/stories/3201.html (accessed 22 March 2006).

8 André Breton, *Nadja*, trans. Richard Howard (London: Penguin, 1999), 64.

9 Pierre Missac, *Walter Benjamin's Passages*, trans. Shierry Weber Nicholson (Cambridge, Mass.: MIT Press, 1996), 179.

10 On the stripping of the drums and the emergence of the clock see Duanfang Lu, *Remaking Chinese Urban Form: Modernity, Scarcity and Space, 1949–2005* (New York: Routledge, 2006), 5. The eight powers were Britain, the United States, France, Russia, Japan, Germany, Italy, and Austria. See also Wu Hung, *Remaking Beijing: Tiananmen Square and the Creation of a Political Space* (Chicago: University of Chicago Press, 2005), 152.

11 Wolfgang Schivelbusch, *The Railway Journey: The Industrialization of Time and Space* (Berkeley: University of California Press, 1986), 22–23.

12 Stephen Kern has gone so far as to say that the scheduling requirements of railways directly necessitated the institution of World Standard Time. See Kern, *The Culture of Time and Space: 1880–1918* (Cambridge, Mass.: Harvard University Press, 1983), 2.

13 Wu, *Remaking Beijing*, 152–153.

14 For further details on the Beijing Telegraph Building, see "Bangeshiji de zhonggou tongxin fazhanshi—Beijing dianbao dalou" (The history of Chinese telecommunication in the past half-century—Beijing Telegraph Building), *Beijing Shangbao* (Beijing Business Today), 21 March 2007, A4.

15 Martin Heidegger, "Origin of Art," in Heidegger, *Basic Writings*, ed. David Farrell Krell (New York: HarperCollins, 1993), 167.

16 Shu Jun, *Tiananmen guangchang lishi dangan* (Historical archives related to Tiananmen Square) (Beijing: Press of the School of the Chinese Communist Party, 1998), 155–156.

17 The number of years needed to increase production to this extent changed during the Great Leap Forward. The initial goal was to overtake Britain in fifteen years and the United States in twenty to thirty. See *Renmin Ribao* (People's Daily), 1 January 1958. In May 1958, when the campaign intensified, the projection changed to seven years to overtake Britain and fifteen years the United States. Soon after that, it became two to three years to overtake Britain; Qi Weiping and Wang Jun, "Guanyu Mao Zedong 'chaoying ganmei' sixiang yanbian-

jieduan de lishi kaocha" (Historical research on the formation and development of Mao Zedong's Thought on surpassing Great Britain and catching up with the United States), *Shixue Yuekan* (Journal of Historical Science), no. 2 (2002).

18 Wu, *Remaking Beijing,* 112.

19 "Dayuejin de chaner" (Children of the Great Leap Forward), *Renmin Ribao* (People's Daily), 25 September 1959, 2.

20 "Shoudu sanshiwanrenci chajia yiwulaodong" (Three hundred thousand citizens participated in volunteer work in the capital), ibid., 26.

21 "Shigeyue chuangzao de qiji" (A miracle made in ten months), ibid., B9.

22 There were a few major exceptions, such as the Capital Gymnasium. Thanks to Geremie R. Barmé for pointing this out.

23 Both Shu Jun (*Tiananmen guangchang lishi dangan,* 61–62) and Jia Yingting (*Tiananmen* [Beijing: China Commercial Press, 1998], 117–118) suggest that faults in the structure of the gate were discovered in the early 1960s and a team was put in place to repair it in 1965. The Cultural Revolution put an end to these reconstruction plans.

24 Yu Min, "Mimi chongjian Tiananmen shimo" (The whole story of the secret restoration of Tiananmen Gate), *Beijing Jishi* (Beijing Chronicle), no. 4 (2005), 60.

25 Ibid., 60–63; Shu Jun, *Tiananmen guangchang beiwanglu* (Recollections about Tiananmen Square) (Beijing: Xiyuan Press, 2005), 41; Lu Bingjie, *Tiananmen* (Jinan: Shandon Pictorial Press, 2004), 66.

26 Minor detailing in the Gate House did change. At the height of the Cultural Revolution, dragon motifs were replaced by sunflowers, which were frequently shown on Mao badges, open and directed toward his face. Thanks to Geremie R. Barmé for this information.

27 Yu, "Mimi chongjian Tiananmen shimo," 62–63.

28 Both Shu (*Tiananmen guangchang lishi dangan,* 61–64) and Jia (*Tiananmen,* 117–119) mention "restoration work" on the gate in 1969 and 1970. Both assert that the work was undertaken under the close personal supervision of Premier Zhou Enlai. Neither mentions Mao or the secrecy surrounding the rebuilding. That element of the restoration project can be found in a short article, "Bimi chongjian tiananmen shimo" (The whole story of the secret restoration of Tiananmen

Gate), circulated on the Internet, for example, http://newchina.com/ zh_cn/domestic/945/20030209/11409294.html (accessed 15 March 2007). Two years later a more detailed story appeared in *Beijing Jishi* (Beijing Chronicle), no. 4 (2005).

29 Declassified Memorandum for the President from Secretary of State William Rogers, "The Possibility of a Soviet Strike against Chinese Nuclear Facilities," 10 September 1969, National Archives, SN 67-69, Def 12 Chicom, http://www.gwu.edu/~nsarchiv/NSAEBB/NSAEBB49/ (accessed 11 March 2007).

30 Luo Dan, "Beijing dixiacheng chang sanshi gongli" (Beijing underground city stretches for thirty kilometers), *Jingbao* (The First), 5 April 2005.

31 Li Jingyi and Tao Li, "Fangkongdong de zuori qingchun" (Yesterday's youth of air-raid shelters), *Beijing Jishi* (Beijing Chronicle), no. 1 (2005), 60.

32 New Year's Day editorial, *Renmin Ribao* (People's Daily), 1 January 1972.

33 For details on the style and architectural inspiration of the new extension wing, see Zhang Bo, "Beijing fandian xinlou" (The new wing of the Beijing Hotel), *Jianzhu Xuebao* (Architectural Journal), May 1974, 18–27. For a more recent "inside story" on the conditions attached to building the new extension wing, see Wang Fan, "Jingdong zhongnanhai de beijingfandian xindonglou shijian" (The incident of the Beijing Hotel new wing that alerted Zhongnanhai), *Zhonghua dushubao* (Chinese Readings), 30 October 2002, 10.

34 Siegfried Kracauer, *The Mass Ornament: Weimar Essays*, trans. Thomas Y. Levin (Cambridge, Mass.: Harvard University Press, 1995), 175.

35 Claude Lefort, *The Political Forms of Modern Society: Bureaucracy, Democracy, Totalitarianism*, ed. John B. Thompson (Cambridge: Polity Press, 1986), 186.

36 Kracauer, *The Mass Ornament*, 182.

37 Ibid., 184.

38 Ibid., 179.

39 Norbert Elias and Eric Dunning, *The Quest for Excitement*, 26, cited in Johan Goudsblom and Stephen Mennell, eds., *The Norbert Elias Reader: A Biographical Selection* (Oxford: Blackwell, 1998), 97.

40 Walter Benjamin, "One Way Street," in Benjamin, *Selected Writings,* vol. 1: *1913–1926,* trans. Edmund Jephcott (Cambridge, Mass.: The Belknap Press of Harvard University Press, 1996), 447.

3 THE COMMUNITY

1 "Ten years of chaos" is a euphemism for the Cultural Revolution, which ran from 1966 to 1976.

2 Gao Wei, *Munhua Beijingcheng* (Random notes on Beijing city) (Beijing: Xueyuan Press, 2003), 169–170.

3 On what she calls the "toilet revolution" see Anne-Marie Broudehoux, *The Making and Selling of Post-Mao Beijing* (London: Routledge, 2004), 182–183.

4 Wang Yuquan, *Laiwuji* (The Laiwu collection) (Beijing: Zhonghuq Shuju, 1983), 47.

5 On the history of Chinese policing, see Michael Dutton, *Policing Chinese Politics* (Durham, N.C.: Duke University Press, 2005).

6 The Five Black Categories were Cultural Revolution terms. They were landlords, rich peasants, antirevolutionaries, bad elements, and right-wingers.

7 For a detailed rundown of the work unit see David Bray, *Social Space and Governance in Urban China: The Danwei System from Origins to Reform* (Stanford: Stanford University Press, 2005).

8 Yi Zhongtian, *Xianhua zhongguoren* (Casually talking Chinese) (Beijing: Hualing Publishing House, 1996), 189; He Xinghan, "People of the Work Unit," in *People and Prose,* ed. Shao Yanxiang and Lin Xianzhi (Beijing: Huachen Publishing House, 1993), 158; Lu Feng, "The Work Unit," *Chinese Social Sciences,* no. 1 (1989), 86.

9 Marcel Mauss, *The Gift,* trans. W. D. Halls (London: Routledge, 1990), 5–6.

10 Ibid., 12.

11 Ibid., 48.

12 Carole Cadwalladr, "The Great Leap Forward [Dispatches]," *Observer Magazine,* 21 January 2007, 35.

4 ETERNAL RETURN

1 Jon Campbell, "Foreign Devil: Yar Matey! Sailing the Pirate-infested Seas of Beijing's CD Shops, or: Piracy: A Defence," http://www.popmatters.com/music/columns/Campbell/060407.shtml (accessed 27 October 2006).

2 www.guangzhou.elong.com/theme/themei48.html, quoted in Jeroen de Kloet, "Popular Music and Youth in Urban China: The Dakou Generation," in *Culture in the Contemporary PRC* (Cambridge: Cambridge University Press, 2005), 95.

3 http://playtherecords.com/2005/11/dakou-real-punks-are-chinese.html (accessed 12 October 2006).

4 De Kloet, "Popular Music and Youth in Urban China," 96.

5 In its early years, admission to the MIDI music festival was always free. More recently, as the event has become increasingly popular, the organizer has had to find larger venues to accommodate rock fans and collect cover charges from the audience. A ticket for all four days cost 100 yuan (thirteen U.S. dollars) in 2007.

6 Friedrich Nietzsche, *The Will to Power*, trans. W. Kaufmann and R. J. Hollingdale (New York: Vintage, 1968), bk. 4, 371.

7 Rhoads Murphey, *Key to Modern China* (Cambridge, Mass.: Harvard University Press, 1953).

8 Chen Guanzhong, "Bohemian Beijing," in *Bohemian China* (Hong Kong: Oxford University Press, 2004), 7.

9 Walter Benjamin, *The Arcades Project*, trans. Howard Eiland and Kevin McLaughlin (Cambridge, Mass.: The Belknap Press of Harvard University Press, 1999), 428.

5 AUTHENTICITY

1 Mark Schilling, *The Encyclopedia of Japanese Pop Culture* (New York: Weatherhill, 1997), 85.

2 Bill Kelly, "Japan's Empty Orchestras: Echoes of Japanese Culture in the Performance of Karaoke," in *The Worlds of Japanese Popular Culture: Gender, Shifting Boundaries and Global Cultures*, ed. D. P. Martinez (Cambridge: Cambridge University Press, 1998), 79.

3 Walter Benjamin and René Girard, quoted in Pang Laikwan's paper "Mimesis and Creation: China Who Makes and Fakes," 6. Thanks to the author for making this document available.

4 Iris, "Beijingren vs. Waidiren" (A Beijinger vs. an outsider), in *Walei Beijing—Xia—Taiwanmei, gaoshawenhuaguancha?* (Walei Beijing—What kind of cultural observation, Taiwan girl?) (Taipei: Hongshuo, 2005), 38.

5 Ibid., 36.

6 Chen Guanzhong, *Bohemian China* (Hong Kong: Oxford University Press, 2004), 34.

7 Yan Jun, in Yin Lichuang et al., "Yaogun jidi: ran women zhuang qilai = The Rock & Roll Camp: Let's Rock," in *Zai beijing shengcun de yibai ge liyou = 100 Reasons to Enjoy Beijing* (Taipei: Dakuai wenhua, 2005), 94.

8 Iris, "Beijingren vs. Waidiren," 93.

9 For an account in English see Anne-Marie Broudehoux, *The Making and Selling of Post-Mao Beijing* (London: Routledge, 2004), 42–84.

10 Italo Calvino, *Invisible Cities*, trans. William Weaver (London: Vintage, 1997), 19.

6 ART MARKET, MARKET ART

1 The market occupies 48,500 square feet and has more than 3,000 stalls; http://www.panjiayuan.com.cn/ (accessed 19 June 2006).

2 They are in this regard like Benjamin's flâneur, collector, and gambler. See "Translators' Foreword" in Walter Benjamin, *The Arcades Project,* trans. Howard Eiland and Kevin McLaughlin (Cambridge, Mass.: The Belknap Press of Harvard University Press, 1999), xii.

3 Most of these urban legends are transmitted by word of mouth, but the tale of Zhao Qingwei and the Cultural Revolution relics can be found in a *New China* press report. See http://news.xinhuanet.com/collection/2004-11/01/content_2162818.htm.

4 Qin Jie, "Cang zai Beijing" (Collecting in Beijing), *Zhonghua dushuwang* (Chinese Readings on the Net), 4 April 2004, http://www.booktide.com/news/20040414/200404140020.html (accessed 30 March 2007).

5 Carl von Clausewitz, *On War,* trans. J. J. Graham (New York: Barnes and

Noble, 1956), bk. 1, chap. 3.

6 Jean Baudrillard, "The System of Collecting," in *The Cultures of Collecting*, ed. John Elsner and Roger Cardinal (Melbourne: Melbourne University Press, 2004), 9.

7 Quoted in Geremie Barmé and Linda Jaivine, *New Ghosts, Old Dreams: Chinese Rebel Voices* (New York: Times Books, 1992), xxvi.

8 Lynn Zhang, "Mao's New Tailor: Sui Jianguo," http://new.artzinchina .com/display.php?a=89 (accessed 19 November 2007).

9 Quoted in Xiao Changyan, "End of an Era," *China Daily*, 16 March 2004, http://www.chinadaily.com.cn/english/doc/2004-03/16/content _315318.htm (accessed 13 May 2007).

10 Rent estimates given here should be treated with caution, as they vary dramatically from one contract to the next. We interviewed one person who still paid only 45 dollars (Chinese) per meter in 2005, and she was on a three-year contract. She informed us that her rent was possibly the cheapest in the compound and that she could easily sublet her space at 120 dollars per square meter. The prices given here are therefore only very rough estimates. The information on 1995 prices is drawn from He Wenzhao, "798 Factory, 798 Art: A Social Experimental Report," in *Beijing 798: Reflections on Art, Architecture and Society in China*, ed. Huang Rui (Hong Kong: Timezone 8 and Thinking Hands, 2004), 32. The 2004 prices are given in Xiao, "End of an Era." Prices in 2007 come from author interviews conducted at 798 in April 2007.

11 He, "798 Factory, 798 Art," 32.

12 Liao Wei-tang, "Re-creating Factory 798," in Chen Guanzhong, *Bohemian China* (Hong Kong: Oxford University Press, 2004), 112.

13 http://www.longmarchspace.com/zlzt/pili/e-lunwen.htm (accessed 15 June 2006).

14 Jean Baudrillard, *Simulacra and Simulation*, trans. Sheila Faria Glaser (Ann Arbor: University of Michigan Press, 1994), 9.

15 Ibid., 13.

16 Sigmund Freud, *Jokes and Their Relation to the Unconscious*, vol. 6 of *The Complete Works of Sigmund Freud*, trans. James Strachey, ed. Angela Richards (Middlesex: Penguin, 1976), 40, 52.

ADDITIONAL SOURCES

For those interested in learning a little more about "our Beijing," we offer below some of the books and other media that have helped us navigate our way through this city, its history and meanings.

On Tiananmen Square the most detailed work in English is by the curator and academic Wu Hung, whose *Remaking Beijing* (Chicago: University of Chicago Press, 2005) intersperses personal reminiscences with discussion of the square's art, architecture, and symbolism. For a similarly detailed work on the Imperial Palace, see Geremie R. Barmé's *Forbidden City* (Cambridge, Mass.: Harvard University Press, forthcoming); and for the personal touch, see the account of the life of Pu Yi, the last Qing Dynasty emperor, in Bernardo Bertolucci's classic 1998 film, *The Last Emperor* (Yanco Films Limited), which is based on Pu Yi's biography, *From Emperor to Citizen* (Beijing: Foreign Languages Press, 2002), and also offers some great shots of the Forbidden City.

For more general guides to Beijing's architecture and its symbolic meaning there are a number of works worthy of attention. The architect Zhu Jianfei has written a rather academic book, *Chinese Spatial Strategies: Imperial Beijing, 1420–1911* (London: Routledge/Curzon, 2003). As the title suggests, this deals with the cosmological elements that underpin the traditional city plan and shows how the plan played a key role in establishing the cosmological basis of imperial power. On the massive architectural and social changes the city has undergone since economic reform, Anne-Marie Broudehoux's *Making and Selling of Post-Mao Beijing* (London: Routledge, 2004) offers a detailed up-to-date guide.

For accounts of power and architecture in Beijing, especially in the socialist period, see Duanfang Lu, *Remaking Chinese Urban Form: Modernity, Scarcity and Space, 1949–2005* (New York: Routledge, 2006), which covers both the monumental and the everyday architecture of the city. On everyday architecture and its symbolic meaning, see David Bray's *Social Space and Governance in Urban China: The Danwei System from Origins to Reform* (Stanford: Stanford University Press, 2005). This deals with the spatial/social arrangements of work units in terms of the utopianism that underpinned the Maoist socialist project. The documentary *Morning Sun* (Longbow Productions, 2003) shows that the Red Guard Movement during the Cultural Revolution, far from being chaotic or self-interested, was often motivated by a political intensity that grew from a commitment to a higher cause. Michael Dutton's *Policing Chinese Politics* (Durham, N.C.: Duke University Press, 2005) shows how Mao's friend/enemy divide led to an intense class struggle that would drive the whole of the Chinese revolution.

On how political commitment feeds into the issue of class struggle, Marcel Mauss's *The Gift* (trans. W. D. Halls; London: Routledge, 1990) and the first volume of George Bataille's *Accursed Share* (trans. Robert Hurley; New York: Zone, 1991), in connection with the Chinese notion of *guanxi* (connectedness), are well worth reading. Mayfair Mei-hui Yang, *Gifts, Favors, and Banquets* (Ithaca: Cornell University Press, 1994), reads *guanxi* alongside the Maussian idea of the gift to shed light on everyday interactions rather than on the politics of the everyday.

Michael Dutton's *Streetlife China* (Cambridge: Cambridge University Press, 1998) shows the way in which the idea of the gift played into the everyday politics of China and provides a good, more detailed, and quirkier complement to some key arguments of this book. For how Mao Zedong fares today, see Geremie R. Barmé's *Shades of Mao* (Armonk, N.Y.: M. E. Sharpe, 1996), which offers a fine collection of documents and discussions about the postreform treatment of the Chairman. For more on other Chinese lives, Sang Ye's wonderful *China Candid: The People of the People's Republic,* edited by Geremie R. Barmé with Miriam Lang (Berkeley: University of California Press, 2006), is a good place to start. Sang Ye's work adds color and wit to any understanding of everyday China through interviews with an unusual assortment of characters, from a Chinese executioner to the head of the Chinese UFO association. For an entirely different plotline, have a look at Zhang Yimo's 1994 film, *To Live* (ERA International), in which he traces the trials and tribulations of one Chinese character from dynastic times until economic reform, plotting this life metonymically alongside the trials and tribulations of the Chinese nation. In some respects, this is not unlike Tian Zhuangzhuang's 1993 movie *Blue Kite* (Longwick Film Productions, Beijing Film Studio), which traces Maoist politics through family-based life stories to focus on the tragedy of the revolutionary period. For more contemporary but no less tragic accounts of life in Beijing there are films such as the tragicomedy *Beijing Bicycle* (Art Light Films and others, 2002), directed by Wang Xiaoshuai; and Zhang Yuan's *Beijing Bastards* (October Pictures, 1993). The latter is a Chinese version of Danny Boyle's *Trainspotting* and should not be missed by anyone interested in contemporary Chinese urban youth. Ethnographically, Ning Ying's *Beijing Trilogy* is also worthy of attention. The second installment of this trilogy, *On the Beat (Min jing gu shi)* (Eurasia Communications, 1995), is a valuable complement to our chapter on community and policing.

Laikwan Pang's *Cultural Control and Globalization in Asia* (London: Routledge, 2006) covers piracy and copyright from a more academic and detailed perspective and, if read alongside the postmodern empiricism of Hillel Schwartz's *Culture of the Copy* (New York: Zone Books, 1996), leaves one wondering what is original, authentic, or genuine in either our world or Beijing's. *Appetites: Food and Sex in Post-Socialist China,* by Judith Farquhar (Durham, N.C.: Duke University Press, 2002), offers an interesting account of food, medicine, and popular culture in contemporary Chinese life.

For more literary accounts of similar trends, we recommend Chun Shu's semiautobiographical novel, *Beijing Doll* (New York: Riverhead Trade, 2004), which depicts the life of a materialistic, cruel, and decadent teenage girl in modern Beijing. For an example of the "bad boy" literature popular among Beijing's rebels, read Wang Shuo's classic "hoodlum novel," *Playing for Thrills* (trans. Howard Goldblatt; New York: Penguin, 1998), or his more recent *Please Don't Call Me Human* (trans. Howard Goldblatt; New York: Hyperion, 2000). For a rundown on the art scene and on Factory 798 in particular, see Eric Eckholm et al., *Beijing 798: Reflections on Art, Architecture, and Society in China* (New York: Timezone 8, 2005).

For those interested in Chinese rock, Cui Jian's "Yi wi suo you" (Nothing to my name) is a classic anthem of the 1980s. In this song Cui, hailed as China's founder of rock, cleverly blends northern Chinese folksong and musical instrumentation with Western-style rock. His music greatly influenced China's rock music in the following decade. Cui's first real album, *New Long March Rock and Roll*, is a must for those curious about Beijing's punk-rock scene. Tang Dynasty, an offshoot of the Cui-pioneered punk-rock movement, is widely regarded as China's first heavy-metal band. Very successful in the 1990s, Tang Dynasty, like Cui, mixes Western-style rock with traditional Chinese vocal techniques. Though a little outdated, both Cui Jian and Tang Dynasty capture the rebellious and bohemian spirit of northern drifters explored in our chapter "Eternal Return." For the most comprehensive book about this punk-rock scene, see Andrew Jones, *Like a Knife*, Cornell East Asian Series, no. 57 (Ithaca: Cornell University East Asian Program, 1992).

ACKNOWLEDGMENTS

This book was a collective effort led by Dutton and researched and executed in Beijing, London, Taipei, and Melbourne by Dutton, Lo, and Wu. Like the Ten Great Projects of which we write, this work was accomplished at breakneck speed and with much enthusiasm. We hope our enthusiasm is infectious, and that we have conveyed something of the intellectual excitement and insight created by the people we talked with and interviewed.

Many people who have contributed mightily to this book are named on its pages, and they are deserving of our special thanks for their participation in this project. But some of the most generous contributors to the text are present there in spirit only. We would like to acknowledge especially those women and men who helped us behind the scenes. Carol Han Zhao and her family found housing for us in Beijing during our research trips. Si Qi gave generously of her time and studio space in 798. Wang Yi offered advice on Beijing's architecture. Yao Yao, Ding Jieming, Jane Huang, Sean Wang, and the Zakka gang kept us in coffee, tea, and food but most of all fed us stories and themes that we followed up. Jerry Liu, Jennie Ku, and Pauline Hsu offered critical research assistance.

Huang Du's curatorial knowledge was a useful aid when we needed to know about the avant-garde art scene in Beijing, and he introduced us to many local artists. Wang Jingsong, Yan Lei, and Zhao Bandi (Pandaman) generously shared their time, their perspectives, and their artwork for reproduction in the book. With the exception of images 15, 23, 28, and 58, all photographs were taken by the authors or by Li Donghan, whose expertise we very much appreciate. We would also like to thank Si Qi, Li Liang, and Valentina Lucaks for supplying additional photographs to enhance the text.

The research on Jiaodaokou would not have been possible without the support of the Ministry of Public Security, the Beijing Public

Security Bureau, and the Police Studies Association of China. Dutton had the honor of being the first ever ethnographer-in-residence at a Beijing police station, and it was from the Jiaodaokou station that much of the research for Chapter 3 was undertaken. Initially funded by an Australian Research Council Grant, that original trip and later follow-up visits were made possible by the good offices of Ma Weigang, who also arranged for Guo Zheng, Gao Enyan, He Dongqing, Li Xueping, Wang Jingtian, Chen Heqing, and Xu Yongqi to offer guidance and advice on areas of special concern to us. Our deepest thanks goes to these citizens of Beijing.

Deborah Kessler has been a source of unending intellectual, practical, and personal support. She advised, encouraged, read drafts, and offered critical comments. She also kept Dutton and Lo fed, housed, and happy, putting up with their idiosyncratic and obsessive work habits and their varied moods. Stacy Lo is grateful to many friends and family members for their love and support. She is especially indebted to her parents, whose generosity is, for her, an invaluable gift. Dong Dong Wu would like to thank Jothi Saunthararajah and Douglas Belford in Melbourne for both moral support and practical assistance that kept her focused on her goals.

Lindsay Waters at Harvard University Press was an intellectual inspiration to us. He commissioned this work, and his verdict on original drafts led us to both tighten our essay and extend it beyond a narrow and orthodox focus. In addition to offering support and encouragement, he chose astute peer reviewers whose valuable advice cautioned against substituting style for substance. Susan Wallace Boehmer, Phoebe Kosman, and the rest of the able team at Harvard University Press worked tirelessly and patiently with us, giving direction at critical moments and making sure we met our deadlines without compromising the integrity of the work that remained to be done. Finally, our special thanks go to Ann Hawthorne, who like the "fifth Beatle," manager Brian Epstein, became our fourth author. She edited out repetitions, polished prose, and called our attention to obscure passages. We are grateful beyond words for her unflagging attention to our manuscript and its needs.

We have traveled a long way since the inception of this project, even if the text itself never leaves Beijing and most of the writing was done in London. Like Marco Polo, we ventured forth on a journey of discovery and wonder, digging out parts of Beijing that we thought would be interesting to our readers. Our hope is that you liked what you found as you joined us on our travels through a city touted to be, in one way or another, central to our collective futures.